RIDING WITH COCHISE

Also by the author:

RIDING WITH COCHISE

The Apache Story of America's Longest War

Steve Price

Skyhorse Publishing

Skyhorse Publishing books may be purchased in bulk at special discounts for sales promotion, corporate gifts, fund-raising, or educational purposes. Special editions can also be created to specifications. For details, contact the Special Sales Department, Skyhorse Publishing, 307 West 36th Street, 11th Floor, New York, NY 10018 or info@skyhorsepublishing.com.

Skyhorse® and Skyhorse Publishing® are registered trademarks of Skyhorse Publishing, Inc.®, a Delaware corporation.

Visit our website at www.skyhorsepublishing.com.

10 9 8 7 6 5 4 3 2

Library of Congress Cataloging-in-Publication Data is available on file.

Cover design by Kai Texel
Cover art credit: "Dusk" by David Nordahl, davidnordahl.com
Photos within, unless otherwise noted, by Steve Price

Print ISBN: 978-1-5107-7457-5
Ebook ISBN: 978-1-5107-7458-2

Printed in China

To Freddie Kay-dah-zinne.

Cochise would have been proud of his great-great-grandson.

Contents

Introduction

Early one bright, windy April morning, my close friend John Walker and I trailered our horses south from Albuquerque to the ruins of old Fort Cummings, located in Luna County about twenty miles north of Deming, New Mexico. We did not come to see the fort, because almost nothing remains of the adobe structures after nearly 150 years of standing abandoned in the harsh New Mexico climate. Instead, we came to see why Fort Cummings was even built.

It was established at 11 p.m. on the night of October 2, 1863, by Captain Valentine Dresher, the commanding officer of Company B, First Infantry of the California Volunteers. He arrived and made camp at a permanent water source named Cooke's Springs, just south of a narrow, rocky four-mile-long break in the mountains named Cooke's Canyon. Both were named by General Philip St. George Cooke, who found them in 1846 while leading Brigham Young's famous Mormon Battalion to California to fight in the Mexican–American War.

By 1863, however, both the water and the canyon were controlled by the Apaches, who were being led by an imposing and charismatic leader named Cochise. Between 1861 and 1863, he and his warriors are said to have ambushed and killed more than a hundred travelers and soldiers (some have put the number closer to four hundred) moving through Cooke's Canyon. The Apaches knew the ancient volcanic peak as Dzil tan a tal, or "Mountain Holds Its Head Up Proudly." It was, and still is, a beautiful, rugged mountain.

By the 1860s, the canyon had become an established shortcut along the primary travel route between southern New Mexico and California, leading through the heart of the Apache homeland. Indeed, because of Cochise, it became known as Massacre Canyon, and even Brigadier General James H. Carleton, the officer who ordered Dresher to construct Fort Cummings, described the canyon as the most dangerous place in all of New Mexico and Arizona.

Fort Cummings was created specifically to control Cochise, and John and I wanted to ride the very same trails he had ridden, touch the same rocks he had touched. It was a chilling experience. In the months preceding our ride, I had hiked deep into the Cochise Stronghold, his home in Arizona's Dragoon Mountains. I had studied the rock cairns marking the gravesites of men the Apaches had killed at Dragoon Springs and had walked through Apache Pass, possibly standing in the very spot where Lieutenant George Bascom tried to take Cochise prisoner, the act that started the chieftain's vicious war against the Americans.

I had ridden horseback in the Gila National Forest, almost certainly following a travel route used by Mangas Coloradas on his way to the Santa Rita del Cobre mines, and Walker and I had traced Victorio's footsteps through his beloved Alamosa Canyon. We had then visited the ruins of Fort Craig, where soldiers had ridden out to fight Victorio and Cochise, as well as to engage General Henry H. Sibley's Confederate troops in the Battle of Valverde on the Rio Grande, where Bascom was killed.

Everywhere I traveled, the ghosts were still present, but in Cooke's Canyon, as we guided our horses slowly around the boulders and along the canyon wall, I kept expecting to see arrows flying through the air and hear gunfire echoing over the rocks. An isolated, elongated mound of small stones to one side almost certainly marked the gravesite of one of Cochise's victims; not that many years ago, the remains of settlers' wagons could still be found in the weeds and gullies at the mouth of the canyon.

The Apache Wars ranged across southern New Mexico and Arizona as well as into both Sonora and Chihuahua, Mexico, but to many, Massacre Canyon is considered one of the epicenters of the fighting: not just because Cochise made it so, but also because he and Victorio, Geronimo, and Mangas Coloradas, the four chieftains I profile in this book, all camped, hid, and fought there.

The canyon perfectly suited the Apache style of fighting, which primarily revolved around sudden, hidden ambushes

Little remains today of Fort Cummings, which was built in 1863 specifically to control Cochise and protect travelers heading through Cooke's Canyon.

when their unsuspecting foes were confined by the geography of the site, be it canyon walls, rivers and streams, or even deep gullies. All the Apache leaders, but particularly Cochise, learned to choose the locations of their ambushes so their own losses would be minimal. When they withdrew, their intimate knowledge of the land allowed them to seemingly disappear at will.

Early in my research, I met Freddie Kay-dah-zinne, an historian for the Chiricahua Apaches, a tribal medicine man, and the great-great-grandson of Cochise. I cannot count the hours we spent together visiting and interviewing on the Mescalero Apache Reservation where he lived. Freddie was extremely gracious with his time and patience in answering my never-ending questions, not just about Cochise but also about the Apache culture in general during that particular time in history.

One day after lunch, in what had become our favorite tribal café, Freddie introduced me to another man whom I had only dreamed of meeting: Harlyn Geronimo, the great-grandson of the famous fighter Geronimo. Like Freddie, Harlyn is also a tribal medicine man, and he was also kind and gracious in talking to me, sometimes for entire afternoons during which time I barely moved in my chair. I took Harlyn and his wife Karen to dinner one night, but do not remember anything I ate because I was mesmerized by Harlyn's stories of his great-grandfather's life, things he admitted he had never told anyone else.

As Freddie had in our earlier conversations, Harlyn and Karen both described how religion played an important role in Apache life. The Apaches worshipped one god whom they called Ussen; many, especially tribal leaders, prayed to him several times daily. The Apaches believed Ussen had only made them caretakers of the Earth, and if they did not care for it properly, it would be taken from them. Thus, it is easy to understand why they instantly disliked the miners who flooded into their homelands with picks and shovels and destroyed the land they were charged to care for.

The Apaches also prayed for help when danger threatened. During our dinner at the Inn of the Mountain Gods in Ruidoso, Harlyn and Karen both described how Geronimo prayed for guidance when he and his band saw a long column of soldiers approaching the mountain where they were hiding. The story had been told to Karen by her grandmother Alberta, who was a young girl with Geronimo when it happened.

Knowing they had no chance to escape, Geronimo told his people to wait for him while he went to the mountaintop to pray. After a short time he returned and told the band to hide

Cooke's Canyon suited the Apache style of ambush fighting because it confined travelers into a relatively narrow area with little chance of escape. Cochise and his warriors are reported to have slain more than a hundred travelers moving through the canyon during a two-year period.

their horses in the rocky draws and behind boulders, and to just sit motionless beside the boulders. This they did, and the soldiers, often riding within twenty feet of the Apaches, never saw them.

Other stories of their unwavering religious faith center around a warrior woman named Lozen, Victorio's sister, who often rode with him and the other Apache men into battle. She had a special power, a gift given to her by Ussen, in which she would be shown where enemy soldiers were located, or the direction from which they were approaching. Lozen, it is said, would hold out her arms and slowly rotate in a circle while chanting a special prayer. When her arms began to tingle and perhaps turn reddish, it meant Ussen was telling her she was pointing in the right direction. Others could recite the same prayer, Kay-dah-zinne emphasized to me, but it would not be answered. Lozen, like Cochise, were themselves gifts to the Apaches from Ussen.

Another with a special god-given gift, or power, was Nana, the crippled warrior who stayed with Geronimo to the final surrender, suffered through his years of imprisonment in Florida and Alabama, and is buried with Geronimo at Fort Sill, Oklahoma. Nana's gift was his ability to locate ammunition for the warriors, and this is what Victorio had sent him to do when the chieftain was surrounded by Mexican soldiers and killed at Tres Castillos in 1880.

Finding ammunition was always a problem for the Apaches because during the years immediately following the Civil War, American cavalry units used various models of carbines in different calibers, and some military units still used percussion cap rifles. A photograph of Geronimo and three of his warriors, taken shortly after his surrender in 1886, shows Geronimo holding an 1873 Springfield long rifle, while two of his companions have 1873 Winchesters and the third holds an 1873 Springfield carbine. Thus, Nana often was forced to steal or trade not only for ammunition but also for weapons that used that particular ammunition. There are stories throughout the Southwest of

Apaches trying to trade as many as two or three horses for a single box of rifle cartridges.

Both Harlyn and Freddie had, over the years, visited many of the battlefields and other sites made famous by their relatives, and their gentle guidance and suggestions certainly helped shape this book. Without their help, I know I would have ridden into more than one dead-end canyon. Walking or riding horseback through the sand, rocks, and greasewood that mark many of those sites today, a casual observer might judge it as land not worth fighting for, but to the Apaches all of it was land given to

This small, isolated mound of rocks in the weeds of Cooke's Canyon quite likely marks the grave of one of Cochise's victims. The four-mile-long break in the mountains became part of the primary travel route for anyone heading west to Tucson or beyond, and the Apaches attacked those travelers so regularly it became known as Massacre Canyon.

them by their god, a lesson they carried with them from their earliest childhood. They had been instructed not only to care for it but to love it, and they did.

The Apache Wars are a tragic story of a people who fought long and hard to keep their homeland and their culture despite decades of betrayal by enemies who never really wanted or seriously tried to understand them. There was vicious fighting from both sides, but there never were a lot of Apaches, and from the beginning they perhaps were destined for defeat. The concept of Manifest Destiny blew across the country like a winter blizzard and brought more Americans onto Apache soil than there were leaves on the cottonwood trees in Alamosa Canyon or rocks on the ground in Massacre Canyon.

When Geronimo finally surrendered in September 1886, his band numbered just thirty-four men, women, and children—the last Apaches who waged war against the United States. For more than five months, this tiny band had outrun and outfought five thousand American soldiers and three thousand additional Mexican troops, who during that nearly half a year never captured a single member of his band. A feat like this is all but incomprehensible in today's world.

In this book, I tell the story of this amazing tribe and their equally amazing but historically elusive leaders. It is as much about a time—during which the longest war the United States has ever been involved in was waged—as it is about any single individual.

When an entire culture is destroyed as thoroughly as was that of the Apaches, the long-term loss to the victor always extends far beyond the casualties on the battleground. Many Apaches were killed or surrendered through the years of fighting, but you can decide whether they truly lost the war.

—Steve Price
Tijeras, New Mexico

CHAPTER 1

A SENSE OF PLACE

It was Tuesday, October 1, 1872, the time of year when nighttime temperatures in the Dragoon Mountains of southeast Arizona were cold but the days sunny and comfortable. Three hours after their dawn breakfast of fried bread and coffee, the men, including one-armed Brigadier General Oliver O. Howard; his aide-de-camp, Lieutenant Joseph A. Sladen; and one of their guides, the red-bearded Thomas J. Jeffords, were likely still sitting by their campfire.

At mid-morning their wait ended abruptly when an Apache warrior carrying a long war spear, his face daubed with black and vermilion dye, galloped full speed into the camp on horseback. Scarcely a dozen feet from the now standing white men, he pulled his horse up, jumped down, and ran to Jeffords, where the two embraced each other warmly like long-lost friends. His name was Juan, Jeffords explained, and he was the younger brother of the man they had come to meet, the chief of the Chiricahua Apaches named Goci, better known to Americans as Cochise.

Minutes later, four others arrived, led by a man wearing a yellow silk handkerchief around his black hair, who rode with unmistakable dignity. He dismounted very deliberately and, like Juan, greeted Jeffords like an old friend. Jeffords turned to General Howard and said, "General, this is the man; this is he." The general extended his hand, and Cochise took it.

For this remarkable description of one of the most momentous meetings between white man and Indian in the entire history of the American West, but especially the Apaches in what would become the states of Arizona and New Mexico, we can thank Lieutenant Sladen. His book, *Making Peace with Cochise: The 1872 Journal of Captain Joseph Alton Sladen* (1997), provides an eyewitness account of the peace negotiations that took place over the next twelve days, there on the rocks and boulders in the Dragoon Mountains.

Cochise and his band of Chiricahua would move to a reservation established specifically for them along the Arizona-New Mexico-Mexico borders, and Jeffords would become their Indian agent. They would immediately halt their attacks against American citizens anywhere on US soil, and in return, the United States military would leave them alone as long as they obeyed these rules.

Specific details were never officially written or otherwise recorded. This was an agreement between two very principled men who trusted each other, and it brought peace to southern Arizona for the first time since 1860. Even after Cochise died in 1874, his oldest son Taza continued to maintain the agreement.

The peace lasted until June 1876, when mindless officials in Washington decided to abolish the Chiricahua Reservation that Howard and Cochise had established and move the band out of their mountainous home into a dry, rattlesnake-infested, and all but worthless chunk of Arizona desert named San Carlos. Other Apaches had already been sent there. The bureaucratic mindset of the time was to concentrate the Indians so they could more easily be managed and controlled. In this case, the move resulted in another full decade of violence between the Apaches and the US Army.

Located a hundred miles north of Tucson, San Carlos was considered the worst duty station in the Arizona Territory even among the military. Water, where it was available, was foul and stagnant. With summer temperatures regularly reaching 115

Pictures of Naiche, the younger son of Cochise, shown here, are most often used in place of Cochise, as there are no known photographs of the Apache chieftain. Cochise is said to have looked similar to Naiche. *Ben Wittick Collection, Palace of the Governors Photo Archives, New Mexico, New Mexico Historical Museum*

degrees Fahrenheit, little more than cactus grew in the blistering sand and rocks, and snakes and scorpions roamed freely during the night. Lieutenant Britton Davis, who would later negotiate one of Geronimo's surrenders, described San Carlos simply as "Hell's forty acres."

Some historians believe Cochise himself started the Apache War on February 4, 1861, at a place known as Apache Pass located just a few miles east of the rocks where he and Howard met. The pass is a seven-mile-long low divide between the Chiricahua and Dos Cabezas Mountains; it is along the shortest route between El Paso and Tucson, and because it had water, wood, and grass, it attracted miners, emigrants, mail carriers, the Butterfield Overland Mail Company, and the American military.

This was also the ancestral homeland of the Chiricahua, and because of Cochise's request, General Howard had included it in their reservation agreement in 1872. On that fateful day eleven years earlier, however, a brash, inexperienced young second lieutenant named George N. Bascom met with the chief and mistakenly accused him of kidnapping a young American boy named Felix Ward.

Even though Cochise volunteered to try to get the boy back—another band of Apaches, the Coyoteros, had abducted him—Bascom was determined to keep the chief and his family hostage until somehow young Ward was recovered. Cochise slit open the tent where Bascom was holding him and managed to escape, but others in his family did not. The next day, Cochise met Bascom under a flag of truce, but nothing was settled, and in retaliation, Cochise's warriors attacked the nearby Butterfield stage station. They killed one attendant and took another, James F. Wallace, hostage. Later that night, the Apaches attacked a wagon train entering Apache Pass, capturing three more Americans, nine Mexicans, and more than a dozen mules. They tied the Mexicans to the wagons and burned everything.

Once more, Cochise tried to negotiate with Bascom, offering Wallace and the three new hostages in exchange for his family. The young lieutenant again refused, and the next day the Apaches killed the four hostages. In response, Bascom released Cochise's wife and infant son, but hanged Cochise's brother Coyuntura and two of his nephews.

As historian Edwin R. Sweeney writes in his introduction to Sladen's published journal, Bascom's actions "aroused a passionate hatred of Americans in Cochise, and touched off the fierce conflict between him and the Americans that was to last throughout the 1860s. His antagonism for Americans became legendary. It mattered little that only a few Americans had betrayed him; he hated them all." Cochise himself is reported to have told General Howard that he put all the blame on Bascom for starting the resulting years of warfare.

This event has gone down in history as the Bascom Affair, and while it escalated the violence between the Apaches and the US military—an intense and bloody revenge and retaliatory type of warfare that would continue across the Southwest for the next quarter century—different bands of Apaches had already been fighting encroachment into their lands for nearly 250 years.

According to the oral traditions of the Apaches, they have always been in this hot, rocky, seemingly endless land of deserts, mountains, and far horizons. They do not believe they migrated southward from Canada or even across the Bering land bridge, as anthropologists hypothesize. In the Apache religion, their god created the world and placed the Apaches in it, specifically at a spot known today as Ojo Caliente, a crystal clear, 110-degree-Fahrenheit warm spring located in a shaded side valley of Alamosa Creek in the upper end of Alamosa Canyon, approximately fifty miles north of what is now the city of Truth or Consequences, New Mexico. The canyon had—and still has—not only water, but also abundant wild game for food as well as rolling mountains for protection.

Historically, Alamosa Canyon, also known as Warm Springs, was visited by all of the great Apache war chiefs at one time or another. It is almost certainly the birthplace of at least one of those chieftains, Victorio, as well as his legendary warrior sister Lozen. An Apache reservation and Indian agency was eventually established there about half a mile from the spring. On April 21, 1877, Geronimo was captured there.

From Alamosa Canyon, according to the oral tradition, other groups of Apaches gradually moved to different areas they believed their god had assigned to them. The Apaches

Alamosa Canyon, also known as Ojo Caliente, or Warm Springs, is considered by the Apaches to be their ancestral home. According to their oral traditions, their god Ussen created the world and put the Apaches there. Over time, different groups of Apaches gradually moved into different areas of the Southwest.

never thought of themselves as a single tribe like the Comanche or Sioux. They were simply groups of related people, and over time, these different bands became known as the Mescalero, the Jicarilla, the Lipan, the Chiricahua, and others. In the case of the Chiricahua, the group was further divided into smaller bands, including the Chihenne, the Chokonens, the Bedonkohes, and the Nednhis, each of whom lived in a different area.

The Chihenne were the largest, and remained at Warm Springs and Alamosa Canyon; the Chokonens settled in the Dragoon Mountains of southeast Arizona, where Cochise rose to fame; the Bedonkohes moved into the Mogollon and Tularosa Mountains along the Gila River in western New Mexico, where Geronimo was born; and the Nednhis eventually migrated into the Sierra Madre Mountains of northern Mexico, where Juh became their last war chief.

This is how the concept of home, or sense of place, became so critically important in Apache beliefs. They did not consider themselves owners of the land, only caretakers of it, and if they did not respect the land, they believed it would be taken away from them. What matters most to Apaches, Keith Basso writes so eloquently in his essay, "Wisdom Sits in Places," contained in Frances H. Kennedy's historical guidebook, *American Indian Places* (2008), is *where* something occurred, not when it occurred.

"Long before the advent of literacy, places served humankind as durable symbols of distant events and as indispensable aids for remembering and imagining them—and this convenient arrangement, ancient but not outmoded, is with us still today," he writes. "What people make of their places is closely connected to what they make of themselves as members of society and inhabitants of the earth . . . if placemaking is a way of constructing the past, it is also a way of constructing social traditions and in the process, personal and social identities."

To better understand how this sense of place has affected the Apache lifestyle over the centuries, I drove from my home near

Albuquerque to the Mescalero Apache Reservation to visit with Freddie Kay-dah-zinne, the director of the Mescalero Museum and Cultural Center and a well-known Apache historian. He was himself a Chiricahua. He was nearing seventy when he and I first met, but was still very active in tribal affairs. He frequently performed certain ceremonies and sang special Apache songs that date back for generations.

He was a big man, with his black hair pulled together in a small, thin ponytail almost hidden under a baseball cap. When he described an oral tradition, he spoke slowly in short, clear sentences and often interjected Apache words, as if to emphasize certain points. In addition to being a tribal medicine man

Alamosa Canyon today still has huge cottonwood trees along part of the old stream shoreline. Because much of the canyon is privately owned today, a lot of the water is used for irrigation.

and one of the few who could still speak fluent Apache, he was also the great-great-grandson of Cochise.

"We call ourselves N'de or Dine, which mean 'the people,'" he began, "but there were many groups of us, and we all had different names, and nearly always those names described where we were from. It was about place more than any other characteristic. There were 'big water people,' 'plains people,' and 'red paint people.'

"Each group had its own identity but we all spoke the same language. There are different ideas on where the word 'Apache' comes from, maybe from another tribe like the Zuni, or from something in Spanish that the white man changed so he could pronounce it.

"I was taught that my people have always been here, that we never came from anywhere else, and you ask, 'How do you know that?' Our answer is that in our ceremonial stories, we talked about dinosaurs and elephants (wooly mammoths) many centuries before the white man arrived. We had words to describe these creatures, but no one believed us until the modern archaeologists found dinosaur bones and elephant bones where we lived."

The land and places the Apache lived is known as Apacheria, a word that shows up on Spanish maps dating as early as 1710. It stretched roughly from the San Andres Mountains east of the Rio Grande in New Mexico westward to present-day Tucson, northward across the Gila and Salt Rivers, and a thousand miles southward into the Mexican states of Sonora and Chihuahua. There were steep mountains, flat-topped mesas and rock-filled canyons, dry deserts and waterless plains, rushing rivers and clear bubbling springs, thick oak and piñon forests, and rolling prairies.

It was, and is, a land of stark contrasts, harsh and unforgiving while at the same time pristine and serene. It was also a land of seemingly endless monetary wealth, especially in the form of gold, silver, and copper. The Apaches, of course, had no use for any of these minerals, but the white man did, and his search for wealth in the ground broke one of the cardinal rules of the Apache religion and thus their sense of place—destroying Mother Earth.

The encroachment for this wealth began in 1540 with the initial exploratory expedition of Francisco Vasquez de Coronado, which took him across the Southwest, through the heart of the Apache homelands in Arizona and New Mexico. Coronado was looking to duplicate the feat Hernando Cortes had accomplished just nineteen years earlier when he defeated the Aztecs in Mexico. Even more recently—in 1533—Francisco Pizarro had conquered the Incas in Peru.

Both of these conquests had resulted in vast fortunes of gold and silver for Spain, and Coronado himself was searching for what had been described to him as the "seven cities of gold," located somewhere in the region he was exploring. There is some indication he encountered his first Indians along the Gila River, but Pedro de Casteneda, the chronicler of the Coronado expedition, spends more time describing Indians they saw the following year, either in far northeast New Mexico, further east in the Texas Panhandle, or slightly further north in Oklahoma.

It is questionable whether these nomads were Apaches, and most historians doubt they were. These tribesmen lived off buffalo, Casteneda wrote, and followed the herds wherever they went. The only Apache tribe in that general region that followed the buffalo were the Lipan. Regardless of whom the explorer may have met, he did not return to Mexico with any of his hoped-for riches. Many, in fact, dubbed his two-year odyssey a complete failure for that reason.

Coronado was followed in 1598 by the conquistador Juan de Onate, who established the first Spanish colony in New Mexico, which he named San Gabriel, at San Juan Pueblo on the Rio Grande, north of what is now the city of Santa Fe. This marked the true beginning of the encroachment, but for the first century after their initial contact, the Apache lifestyle remained largely unchanged except for one major and profound difference. Sometime early in the seventeenth century, perhaps within a dozen years of Onate's arrival, the Apaches acquired their first horses.

Many believe those horses came from one or more of the Pueblo tribes that were being subjugated by the Spanish to work for them as they took over the pueblos. This forced labor included caring for horses and, in many instances, learning to ride them. Even though King Carlos V of Spain had earlier banned the enslavement of natives, his decree was broken with regularity. The practice grew into a lucrative slave trade that continued for more than two centuries and included Apaches who were frequently taken as children and sold in Mexico.

For the most part, the Apaches learned to stay away from the Spanish missions because of fear of enslavement, but they still met clandestinely with the Pueblos, who gave or traded horses to them and probably showed them how to ride. It did not take the Apaches long to learn how to manage horses themselves, and within a few years they were among the finest horsemen North America has ever produced.

With horses came a new sense of power, freedom, and wealth. Because they were now more mobile, they could raid easier and faster for things they needed. Both the Pueblos and the Spanish became primary targets for cattle, horses, various foods, fire-arms, and pretty much whatever else they could grab on the run. When the Pueblo tribes successfully revolted against the Spanish in 1680, thousands of head of Spanish cattle and horses were simply turned loose, and the Apaches certainly captured their share as the Spanish retreated southward to El Paso and beyond.

The Spanish returned to New Mexico a dozen years later, but by then the Apaches had become not only highly skilled raiders but adept traders as well. The very things they raided for became valuable trade items, and vast trading networks between tribes spread both northward through the Rockies and southward into the Mexican states of Sonora and Chihuahua.

Something else became part of the Apache culture during this time, which was a style of retaliatory warfare. A raid for cattle by the Apaches, for instance, might lead to a military retaliation by the victims, such as the Mexicans (and later, the Americans). When this happened, and particularly if an Apache life was lost, the band retaliated in force. This is exactly how Cochise reacted when Lieutenant Bascom refused his offer to exchange Butterfield Overland Mail employee James Wallace for his relatives.

On April 11, 1821, when Mexico gained its independence from Spain, the moment signaled not only the end of Spanish rule in the Southwest, but also the real beginning of the American encroachment into Apacheria. Prior to this date, Spain had prohibited any serious relations between New Mexico and the United States. Adventurers, explorers, and other Americans were often imprisoned if caught trespassing.

The first to arrive in New Mexico after independence were men like William Becknell, who blazed the trail from Missouri to Santa Fe with a wagon train filled with trade goods. He arrived on November 16 of that year, quickly sold his goods, and headed back to Missouri for more. In so doing, as David Weber notes in *The Taos Trappers* (1968), Becknell became known as the father of the Santa Fe trade. His route became the Santa Fe Trail.

Becknell's group was followed just two weeks later by John McKnight, Thomas James, and a group of trappers who planned to search for beaver throughout the southern Rockies. The village of Taos, located about seventy miles north of Santa Fe, had been a popular jumping-off point for Spanish trappers for more than a century, due to its close proximity to a number of major rivers and their tributaries flowing south out of Colorado. After the region was opened to American trappers, many of the mountain men who were working the northern Rockies ventured south to Taos to spend their winters.

In *The Taos Trappers*, a richly detailed history of the fur trade in the Southwest, Weber quotes Harvey Fergusson's 1927 work, *Wolf Song*, which describes some of the attractions Taos offered to the mountain men: "Taos was a place where corn grew and women lived. Sooner or later every man in the mountains came to Taos. They came to it from as far north as the Red and as far south as the Gila. They came to it like buffalo to a salt lick across thousands of dangerous miles. Taos whiskey and Taos women were known and talked about on every stream in the Rockies. More than any other place, Taos was the heart of the mountains."

The Apaches, along with several other tribes, including the Utes and Comanches, also came to Taos, but for a different reason. Several times a year, mainly in mid to late summer, the tribes came to trade. The largest gatherings were dangerous, often short-tempered extravaganzas during which hundreds of horses, mules, weapons, tools, pots, hides, baskets of food, captured enemy slaves, and bottles of local whiskey—known as Taos Lightning—exchanged hands. Even though the tribes, and especially the Apaches, disliked dealing with Mexicans, a peace was declared during the days of the Fair.

The Apaches hated the Mexicans, particularly those in Sonora, where by 1835 the government was paying bounties for any Apache scalp, even those of women and children; their stated policy was one of genocide of the Apaches. Efforts to establish peace were repeatedly refused by Mexican officials. Other times, tribal members were brought in under the guise of establishing a treaty, then murdered.

This continued for years, with both sides showing no quarter. Cochise's father is believed to have been killed this way, for example, and on March 5, 1851, in a similar raid on a peaceful Apache encampment, the mother, wife, and three children of Geronimo were killed. For the rest of their lives, both Cochise and Geronimo harbored a fierce hatred for any Mexicans, regardless of where they encountered them.

In 1846, the United States began waging its own war with Mexico, defeating them two years later after a strange, hard-fought, but largely misunderstood conflict known to history as the War with Mexico. In defeat, the Treaty of Guadalupe Hidalgo conceded some 525,000 square miles of Mexican territory to the United States.

Although the Apaches at this time had no comprehension of such boundaries, they would be affected throughout the remainder of the century by Mexico's defeat. The land Mexico gave up included most of the present-day states of New Mexico, Arizona, Utah, Nevada, California, and parts of Colorado and Wyoming—not quite all of Apacheria.

Ever since the presidency of Thomas Jefferson and the Lewis and Clark expedition to explore Jefferson's Louisiana Purchase, Americans had begun believing in a romantic notion that came to be known as Manifest Destiny, in which the United States was destined to expand its control over all the territory between the Mississippi and the Pacific. Nothing could have established the course of history more for the Apaches and, indeed, all the nomadic tribes of the American West. The 1846 War with Mexico was largely driven by Manifest Destiny.

The credit for coining the term Manifest Destiny is given to several individuals, but primarily to John O'Sullivan in 1845. O'Sullivan wrote an editorial in the July-August issue of the *Democratic Review* using the term to urge readers (primarily Congress) to advocate for westward expansion. At practically the same time, a similar article appeared in the New York *Morning News*, and since O'Sullivan was the editor of both publications, most believe he wrote it, as well.

The Gadsden Purchase of 1854, in which the United States obtained more than twenty-nine thousand additional square miles of southern Arizona and southwestern New Mexico, provided the final huckleberry, or last nail in the coffin, for the Apaches. The United States wanted the land for the construction of a transcontinental railroad, and Mexico was willing to sell because the country was in financial and political turmoil under the presidency of former military general Antonio Lopez de Santa Anna. The price was $10 million.

The acquisition included land west of the Rio Grande and south of the Gila River, quite probably the birthplaces of two Apaches who would play prominent roles in future relations with the Americans, Mangas Coloradas and Geronimo. It also included the Dragoon Mountains that Cochise would call home.

Each of these events contributed in part to the decades of warfare that were to follow across the Southwest. Explorers,

When they were on the move, which was frequently, the Apaches built very simple shelters like this one out of available brush and grass, known as wikiups. When forced to leave quickly, they simply left them behind.

settlers, and prospectors, all looking for a new start in life or to strike it rich, poured into Apacheria. Mining was particularly encouraged by the American government, regardless of where the riches lay. In the years immediately following the Civil War, the country was on the verge of bankruptcy and desperate for all the gold it could get to pay down the war debt. Whenever gold or silver was discovered in Apacheria, even more outsiders flooded in to stake their claims.

Not only the Apaches but also the Comanches and other tribes had no choice but to resist, as they watched the land change before their eyes. Less than five years after the signing of the Treaty of Guadalupe Hidalgo, the army had spent an estimated $12 million and posted nearly eight thousand troops along the new border with Mexico in efforts to protect the wagon trains filled with new settlers. Fort Buchanan, along Sonoita Creek in southern Arizona, had been established on November 17, 1856, and because the fort brought a measure of stability of the area, even more miners and settlers came in.

To make matters even worse, General William Tecumseh Sherman, who in the summer of 1866 was named commander of the Military Division of the Missouri, seriously doubted any lasting peace between the whites and Indians could be achieved. In his view, Indians should either be killed outright or confined to reservations of the army's choosing.

Years later, Sherman, frustrated with his army's inability to get the Apaches under control, would be quoted as saying that they ought to have another war with Mexico to make them take back the land—and the Apaches—they'd conceded back in 1846.

The Apache sense of place was essentially their culture, explained Freddie Kay-dah-zinne. Because this tribal sense of place formed such a major part of their religion as well as their entire lifestyle, it was only natural the Apaches fought so hard to keep it. "The Indians were fighting to halt the increasing intrusion of whites into their hunting grounds," write Bob

Drury and Tom Clavin in *The Heart of Everything* (2013).

"The simplicity of this oft-stated purpose eluded Sherman. The Army never understood the chieftains they were fighting," the authors continue, "nor Indian warfare in general. Some generals never learned that the strategies employed at Bull Run or Gettysburg would not work in the Southwest."

It is worth noting, perhaps, as Drury and Clavin point out, that American–Indian warfare did not originate with the Apaches. That warfare really began on April 21, 1607, the first time European emigrants set foot in the New World. On that day, Captain Christopher Newport led about twenty of the first permanent English settlers ashore near what was to become Virginia's Jamestown Colony.

After a full day of exploring the immediate area without seeing any other human beings, they were ambushed by Indians, with two men being wounded by arrows.

Freddie Kay-dah-zinne related another story out of the Chiricahua oral history. "There was an Indian," he recited, "who was sitting high on a mountain far way. This Indian said he looked toward the sun and he saw a little bug coming from far, far away, where the sun was coming up in the east. The bug was yellow, like the color of the sun, and it was moving closer and closer and closer. Then he saw that the bug was hairy. "And he saw that the bug started to build something like a web all around him. Slowly, then all of a sudden, he was closed in. He was trapped. He realized he was being placed on a reservation and that the little hairy bug was a white man."

CHAPTER 2

THE AMERICANS: MAJOR GENERAL OLIVER OTIS HOWARD AND TOM JEFFORDS

O f the many varied and historical figures who took part in the Apache Wars, the role Major General Oliver Otis Howard played is frequently overlooked. He is far better known for his gallantry in the Civil War and, two years after his historic meeting with Cochise, for forcing Chief Joseph and the Nez Perce to surrender. Some accounts of Howard's life devote only a sentence or two to his time with the Apaches in the Southwest, possibly because his time with Cochise was so brief.

Although the actual time Howard, Sladen, and Cochise spent together was brief, it was significant. It proved whites and Apaches could live together if each respected the other. Their agreement, as informal as it may seem, brought peace to southern Arizona for the first time since 1860, and might have served as a model for any future Indian–white negotiations. Apache raids ended immediately, and the peace remained in effect for three and a half years. Even after Cochise died on June 8, 1874, his son Taza continued to honor the agreement.

Tom Jeffords, the white man who took Howard to meet Cochise, later wrote, "I doubt if there is any person that could have been sent here that could have performed the mission as well; certainly none could have performed it better."

Born November 8, 1830, in Leeds, Maine, Howard attended Bowdoin College and afterward West Point, where he graduated fourth in his class in 1854. Among his classmates, whom he would fight against later, was J. E. B. Stuart. In 1857, as a second lieutenant and chief of ordnance, Howard was assigned to Fort Brook, Florida, where he took part in fighting the Seminoles. It was during this time, while attending a Methodist tent revival, that he became a devout Christian and his beliefs changed. He returned to West Point later that year and began teaching mathematics, while at the same time working seriously as a Christian evangelist. He was on the verge of resigning his commission to enter the ministry when the Civil War began.

Howard, by then a colonel, commanded a brigade of the Third Maine Volunteers at the first Battle of Bull Run in July 1861, and a few weeks later was promoted to brigadier general. On June 1, 1862, while leading a charge of a brigade of the Sixty-First New York Volunteer Infantry in the Battle of Fair Oaks in Virginia (also known as the Battle of Seven Pines), he was wounded twice in his right arm, which had to be amputated. For his gallantry despite his wounds, he was awarded the Congressional Medal of Honor.

By August, Howard had recovered well enough to rejoin the Army of the Potomac at Antietam, a bloody, tactically inconclusive one-day engagement in Sharpsburg, Virginia, in which 22,717 men died. He was promoted to major general on November 29, 1862, and with the Army of the Potomac fought at Fredericksburg on December 13 that same year. Five months later, Howard assumed command of XI Corps, and although he was outmaneuvered and defeated by Stonewall Jackson at Chancellorsville in May, he moved north to Gettysburg, where he helped position the defenses against assaults by both Jubal Early and George Pickett at Cemetery Ridge.

Howard later commanded the Army of the Cumberland, and in the summer of 1864 took command of the Army of the Tennessee, where he joined Sherman's attack on Atlanta and subsequent March to the Sea. By the end of the war in April 1865, he had a brevet rank of major general.

Even though he had been tested repeatedly in some of the Civil War's bloodiest engagements, Howard frequently based his military decisions on his religious beliefs and required his troops to attend Bible classes, leading to his reputation and nickname as the "Christian General." This was partly why President Andrew Johnson named him to lead the Freedmen's Bureau after the war. The bureau was tasked with integrating former slaves into southern society, and tried to do so by creating schools, providing medical services, and helping the former slaves find employment.

Howard helped establish Howard University in Washington in 1867, and later served as its president. The university had been established specifically to train Black lawyers, doctors, and teachers.

Still serving in the army, Howard was named as Special Indian Commissioner on July 5, 1872, and ordered by then president Ulysses S. Grant to Arizona and New Mexico to negotiate a peace treaty with the Apaches. Attempts to negotiate a truce with Cochise the previous year had failed, despite the fact the Chiricahua leader had voiced his desire for peace. He had not forgotten what Lieutenant Bascom had done to him or his family and still did not trust any American military personnel.

Three years earlier, President Grant had accepted the suggestions of a group of Quakers for pursuing peace with the Apaches, and because his previous attempts had failed, the Quaker recommendations became known as Grant's Peace Policy. At that time, the Quakers were among the most influential religious sects in America, and Grant needed their support.

Grant chose Howard to be his spokesman. The president, of course, knew the general from the war, and the Quakers knew Howard through his evangelism and work with the Freedman's Bureau. Howard's orders were brief and succinct: use his own judgement for terms, but make peace with Cochise.

Major General Oliver Otis Howard lost his right arm during the Civil War in June 1861, but recovered and continued through the rest of the war. He remained in the army, and in 1872 then president Ulysses S. Grant sent Howard to Arizona specifically to negotiate a treaty with Cochise, which he did. *Arizona Historical Society*

Howard and his aide, Lieutenant Joseph A. Sladen, arrived at Fort Apache, Arizona, on August 10 and remained there until August 30, hoping to make contact with Cochise. Sladen, an English emigrant, had fought at Chancellorsville and Gettysburg and been awarded the Medal of Honor for his actions during the Battle of Resaca, Georgia. He'd been part of Howard's staff for a number of years and knew the general well.

They had no success reaching Cochise during their stay at Fort Apache and moved east to Fort Tularosa, New Mexico, arriving on September 4. They'd been told they might find the Chiricahua chief there or, if he was not present, to look for a white man named Jeffords who could lead them to Cochise.

At that particular moment in history, Jeffords was probably the only white man anywhere who could ride into the Dragoon Mountains where Cochise lived and expect to come out alive. His full name was Thomas Jeffords (some historians say his middle name was Jonathan while other say Jefferson; his tombstone just has the letter J) and he was forty when he met Howard. There are many gaps in his story but his close friendship with Cochise is not one of them. He never married, did not write any memoirs, and gave very few interviews.

He was born on New Year's Day 1832, in Chautauqua, New York, the son of Eber and Almira Jeffords. He grew up there and in Ashtabula, Ohio, on the shores of Lake Erie. One biographer, Doug Hocking, notes it is likely Jeffords spent some time sailing schooners on Lake Erie, but by 1858 when he was twenty-six, Jeffords had worked his way to Denver, then known as Cherry Creek, where he made his first ventures into prospecting for gold.

He was in Taos, New Mexico, in 1859 and in Arizona the next year, following one short-lived gold rush after another. By 1861 he was back in New Mexico near Pinos Altos (north of today's Silver City), prospecting the area that would, in just a few years, become almost as well known as an Apache battle-ground as for its minerals.

Stories vary about how and when Jeffords first met Cochise and how their friendship developed. One account, which is highly unlikely, states that after the government shut down the Overland Mail service in 1861, Jeffords was named a supervisor when the US Post Office Department awarded its own contract for mail service between Mesilla, New Mexico, and Tucson in March 1867. These accounts go on to say that Cochise and his warriors were attacking and killing so many of his mail carriers that Jeffords rode alone into the Dragoon Mountains to make his own peace with Cochise.

Another questionable account says Jeffords rode into Cochise's camp to ask for permission to prospect in Cochise's general area. A variation of this, which certainly might be true, was told to well-known historian Eve Ball by Asa Daklugie, son of the Apache chief Juh, who fought alongside Cochise. Daklugie said Cochise's scouts captured Jeffords while he was prospecting and were so impressed by his courage and bravery they spared his life and instead took him to Cochise themselves. Jeffords had by this time learned to speak the Apache language, which undoubtedly impressed Cochise.

"My father (Juh) knew both Cochise and Jeffords well, and he believed the latter account to be true," Ball quotes Daklugie in her book, *Indeh: An Apache Odyssey* (1980). "He knew that the two became very close friends; and in time Juh and Jeffords did, too. Cochise had shut himself off from White Eyes since the Bascom Affair, and accepting a white man as his friend was a tribute to a brave man. No greater praise could be given Jeffords than to say that he won the friendship of Cochise."

Three days after their arrival at Fort Tularosa, on Saturday, September 7, Howard and Sladen had their first sight of Jeffords when he rode into the fort leading a company of cavalry in from patrol. Sladen describes the moment in *Making Peace with Cochise*: "Riding by the side of the commanding officer was a tall, slender citizen, with a long flowing beard of reddish hue, his face shaded by the broad brim of a drab slouch hat, but with a pleasant face lighted up with a pair of bright, piercing eyes of light blue. I looked at this man with considerable curiosity, for this was Jeffords, the man who was to take us to Cochise, if any man could."

Even more revealing is Sladen's journal entry recounting the first conversation between Howard and Jeffords: "I understand, Mr. Jeffords, that you know Cochise, and can find him," writes Sladen. "I have come here from Camp Apache to find you, and if possible, to get you to go to him and induce him to come to me, for an interview."

Jeffords eyed him closely, as if he would read his thoughts, and after a considerable deliberation, puffing the smoke of his cigar slowly as he thought, he took out his cigar and said very deliberately, "General Howard, Cochise won't come. The man that wants to talk to Cochise, must go where he is."

"Do you know where he is?" said the general.

"I can find him," Jeffords laconically replied.

"Will you go to him, with a message from me?" asked the general.

"General," replied Jeffords, with the faintest appearance of a cynical smile. "I'll tell you what I'll do. I will take you to Cochise."

Jeffords, Howard, Sladen, and two additional Chiricahua guides left Fort Tularosa on September 13, reaching Cochise's West Stronghold on September 30. They met Cochise on the morning of October 1, and because the chieftain needed to confer with each of his sub-chiefs about terms of a possible peace agreement, Howard left that same afternoon for Fort Bowie to issue orders that these Apache leaders were not to be attacked, taken prisoner, or otherwise harmed or harassed as they came into the Stronghold, some from as far away as Sonora and Chihuahua in northern Mexico.

Howard returned on October 3 and he and Sladen stayed with Cochise through October 12, when their formal peace agreement was finalized several miles away at an old stage

Tom Jeffords is known to be one of the few, if not the only, white men Cochise ever trusted. General Howard could never have approached him without Jeffords's help. This portrait is believed to have been taken about 1895. *PhotCL 7(25), the Horatio Nelson Rust Collection, The Huntington Library, San Marino, California.*

station at Dragoon Springs. They left that same afternoon and arrived in Tucson on the fourteenth, where they remained for the next several weeks. His entire visit with the great Apache chief had lasted less than two weeks, and neither he nor Sladen is believed to have ever seen Cochise again.

In 1874, Howard was given command of the Department of the Columbia, headquartered at Fort Vancouver on the Columbia River in Washington. In 1876, he fought the Battle of Clearwater with Chief Joseph, but even though his forces outnumbered the Nez Perce more than five to one, the Indians escaped. Howard pursued but had no more direct engagements, and Chief Joseph actually surrendered to General Nelson A. Miles in Montana.

Howard left Fort Vancouver in 1880 to become the superintendent of West Point, where he remained for the next two years. He retired from the army in 1894 with the rank of major general and died on October 26, 1909 in Burlington, Vermont. He is buried there at Lakeview Cemetery.

Lieutenant Sladen stayed with General Howard after their meeting with Cochise and served as his adjutant throughout the Nez Perce campaign. In 1885, when Sladen was assigned back to Fort Vancouver, he and Howard had been together for twenty-two years. In 1888, Sladen was promoted to captain, and retired the next year. He became general manager of Aetna Life Insurance Company and later worked for the German American Insurance Company. He died in Portland on January 25, 1911.

Tom Jeffords served as the Indian agent for the Chiricahua Reservation Cochise and Howard had established, remaining in close contact with the chief until Cochise's death in 1874. A small portion of his office and living quarters is still visible at Apache Pass along the hiking trail leading to Fort Bowie.

When a group of already drunk Apaches killed Nicholas Rogers and Orisoba Spence on April 7, 1876, for refusing to sell them more whiskey, the decision was made in Washington to close the Chiricahua Reservation and move the remaining Indians to San Carlos. Some, including Juh and Geronimo who had fled to Mexico, scattered to other sanctuaries, but the band originally under Cochise went to San Carlos.

Jeffords returned to his earlier love, prospecting and mining, as he knew that the entire region, including Apache Pass, was rich in minerals. He'd actually invested in a number of mines while employed at the Chiricahua Reservation, and for the next several years he worked at a variety of claims with different partners. He also continued to help maintain peace among the Apaches still at San Carlos.

In 1892, he purchased a small ranch and built a home about thirty miles north of Tucson. He continued his mining on a small scale until his death on February 19, 1914. He is buried in the Evergreen Cemetery in Tucson.

CHAPTER 3

PLACES TO SEE:
COCHISE STRONGHOLD

The Cochise Stronghold is the name given to a portion of the Dragoon Mountains where Cochise and his followers lived. The Dragoons, located just west of the city of Benson, Arizona, in the Coronado National Forest, stretch north to south about thirty miles and today remain a fiercely rugged and harsh landscape of steep, rocky cliffs and boulders that fall away into cool, hidden basins. The Stronghold contained water, wild game and other foods, and grazing areas for horses. Most of all, the mountains offered protection.

From the high ramparts, warriors could see for miles in every direction, literally knowing days ahead of time when danger might be approaching. Cochise is believed to have been born here; he met General Howard and Tom Jeffords here; and he is buried here, although the exact site is unknown.

Two canyons, one on each side of the mountains but which nearly meet, offered access into the Stronghold, or escape from it. These same two canyons provide visitor access today to what are commonly called the East Stronghold and the West Stronghold.

The East Stronghold is more developed, and can be reached by taking Exit 331 (Highway 191) from I-10 and following this paved and well-marked road south for eighteen miles to the town of Sunsites. Turn west on Ironwood Road. After five miles Ironwood becomes a gravel road and leads three more miles to the East Stronghold campground. This is a small, oak-shaded campground with only eleven overnight sites (no water is available) and is closed annually from June 1 to September 1 due to fire danger.

Day hiking is still permitted during the summer, however, and an easy four-tenths-mile nature trail leads through the mixed forest of juniper, manzanita, and agave, all marked with identifying signs. Spectacular views of East Stronghold open at every turn of the trail, and at about the halfway point, the

Cochise and his band lived in the Dragoon Mountains of southeastern Arizona, in an extremely rugged area known as the Stronghold. From the higher pinnacles, Apache lookouts could see for miles and know days in advance if an enemy was approaching. Cochise is believed to have been born here.

route intersects the seven-mile Cochise Trail that leads over the mountains into the West Stronghold.

The West Stronghold entrance is reached by driving south on US Highway 80 from Benson for eighteen miles (approximately a mile north of Tombstone) and turning east on Middlemarch Road. The pavement here changes to dirt and gravel after a mile or so, but continue for ten miles until entering the national forest. Signs mark the forest boundary; turn left immediately onto FS Road 687. A four-wheel-drive will be necessary here after rain, and a high clearance vehicle will always be recommended.

Follow FS 687 for six miles and look for FS 687K leading into the brush to the right. This quarter-mile road leads to a

The exact rocks where Cochise and General Howard sat to discuss the Chiricahua Reservation cannot be identified positively, but most believe they looked similar to these rocks (and might have been these) located near the spot known today as Council Rocks near the western entrance into the Stronghold.

small parking lot at the foot of Council Rocks, thought to be the spot where Cochise and General Howard agreed to a peace treaty. There are a lot of big, flat boulders where the two could have sat, but follow the faint trail up to the huge rocks above and start looking for pictographs. The oldest and faintest were created by the Mogollon culture nearly a thousand years ago.

Continue north along FS 687 for another half mile and turn right onto FS 688. A fence and private property mark the end of FS 687. Follow the very rough, rocky road for three miles to its end in a small parking area. Across the dry creek bed is the Cochise Trail trailhead leading approximately seven miles through the mountains to the East Stronghold. The chief's primary campground was on this western side, probably not far from the trail.

CHAPTER 4

THE APACHES:
MANGAS COLORADAS

Of the two men studying each other face to face that warm early August day in 1826, it would have been hard to determine who may have been more interested, or impressed, with the other. One was an unusually tall, magnificently proportioned Apache chieftain likely seeing his first white American; the other a bearded, buckskin-clad fur trapper fully a foot shorter than the well-armed man now standing before him.

The white man was James Ohio Pattie, who with his father Sylvester (sometimes spelled Sylvestre) had left Missouri and come to New Mexico, where they secured the necessary licenses to trap beaver on the Gila River. They, along with the men who had traveled with them, are believed to be the first Americans to attempt to trap the river.

Pattie recorded the meeting in his 1831 book, *The Personal Narrative of James Ohio Pattie of Kentucky*, but does not specifically name any of the chieftains present. Historians generally agree the tall chieftain in charge at that time was an Apache named Fuerte, who in a few years would become far better known as Mangas Coloradas.

The Spanish had explored the Gila more than seventy years earlier, and in 1757 when one of those explorers, a Jesuit priest named Father Bartholome Saenz, described the river to his contemporaries as a place where "beavers gnaw and throw to the ground the alter-trees and cotton woods," it became only a matter of time before the American mountain men found it.

The Spanish, even from the earliest explorations of Coronado, never truly exploited the fur trade themselves. Beaver, regardless of how plentiful they were, did not interest them. They were far more impressed with the soft, tanned deer and elk hides produced by the native tribes, and they traded regularly for them. The Spanish had come to Nuevo Mexico for gold and silver, and to convert the natives to Christianity.

Around 1800, the Spanish found the mineral wealth they had so long craved: this time not gold or silver, but copper. This was in the heartland of the Chihenne band of the Chiricahua, and many believe it was a tribal member who led a Spanish military officer, Lieutenant Colonel Jose Manuel Carrasco, to the site. It was a small forested valley nestled in the mountains about six miles northeast of the present-day town of Bayard.

Carrasco, even though he was not a miner, immediately recognized the riches literally lying in plain view on the ground before him. On June 30, 1801, he filed a claim on the site and began working it himself. He is reported to have collected enough copper to have made at least one very successful and profitable deposit in Chihuahua.

His military duties, however, prohibited him from continuing to exploit his claim, and his inexperience as a miner became apparent in 1804, when he sold the claim to a miner far more qualified to develop it, Francisco Manuel de Elguea. By this time, a small settlement, Santa Rita del Cobre, had been established for those working the mines, and Spanish troops had taken up permanent residence in the valley.

For several years, the Apaches tolerated this Spanish presence. Mangas Coloradas and others visited the settlement often to trade or receive rations—the Spanish way of keeping peace with them—but by 1807 relations had started to sour as more and more miners came to work in the valley.

Spanish archives reveal that Elguea soon began melting the copper, pouring it into ingots weighing 150 pounds each, and transporting them by mule to Chihuahua and from there to Mexico City. Each mule carried two ingots, and many mule trains consisted of as many as a hundred animals.

The Royal Mint in Mexico City contracted with Elguea to purchase the entire output from Santa Rita del Cobre for use in minting coins, paying him 65 centavos per pound of copper delivered to the mint. By 1807, the mine was estimated to be producing six million pounds of copper each year, and when Elguea died, his widow leased the mine to Juan Ortiz, who continued its operation.

The increased activity led to more conflicts and flare-ups with the Apaches. Mangas Coloradas and his band began attacking the returning mule trains, since they were usually loaded with food and other supplies, and on occasion attacked the settlement of Santa Rita itself.

In the decades before Mangas was born, especially during the 1770s while the American colonies far to the east were fighting their own revolution, the Apaches had waged a vicious war against the Spaniards, stealing tens of thousands of head of livestock and forcing dozens of ranches in northern Sonora and Chihuahua to be abandoned. An uneasy peace had been established when the Spanish military, realizing its inability to control the raiding, finally responded with treaties that provided rations, primarily meat as well as clothing and even firearms.

The idea was to provide the very items the Apaches were raiding for so they would have no further reason to conduct their bloody raids. In turn, to receive these supplies, the Apaches had to agree to live peacefully in close proximity to the Spanish distribution points, which were presidios, garrisons where military forces were stationed.

The system, despite its flaws, worked until about 1795 when war broke out between Spain and France, forcing Spain to end its subsistence program for the Indians. Apache raids became

There are no known photographs of Mangas Coloradas, but he is thought to have looked similar to his youngest son Mangus, shown here. Born about 1840, Mangus fought actively with Geronimo after his father's death. He was imprisoned in Florida and then at Fort Sill, Oklahoma, but moved to the Mescalero Reservation in Oklahoma when allowed to go. *Credit: Ben Wittick Collection, Palace of the Governors Photo Archives, New Mexico Historical Museum*

even more frequent after Mexico gained its independence from Spain in 1821 and Spanish troops, especially those stationed in the states of Sonora and Chihuahua, were removed. When Mexico began permitting foreigners into the country and allowing them to exploit the new land and its resources, Apache resistance against Mexico became even stronger.

This is what James O. Pattie, his father Sylvester, and their band of trappers walked into when they arrived at Santa Rita that summer day in 1826. Ortiz, unable to defend Santa Rita against the raids, leased the mine to the elder Pattie.

Within two years, Sylvester had accumulated some $30,000 in profits, but he lost it all in April 1827, when he sent one of his workers to Santa Fe with the money and instructions to purchase additional equipment to continue operating the mine. The worker never showed up in Santa Fe, and subsequent attempts to locate him failed. Pattie and his son, financially devastated and without funds to continue mining, left and returned to Santa Fe and the fur trade.

Mangas Coloradas was immediately impressed with Pattie and the other Americans with him, whereas he felt nothing but disdain for the Spanish and the Mexicans. He pledged peace to the Americans and even to those Mexicans working with them in the mines. The Apache leader could see how organized they were and, more importantly, that they treated the Apaches fairly and with respect.

After Sylvester and James Pattie left, and Ortiz was forced to return to Spain, several different operators continued to manage Santa Rita del Cobre. By now it was actually a series of mines throughout the valley, but by 1834, under nearly constant attack by the Apaches, Santa Rita was abandoned.

Today, more than a century and a half later, the Santa Rita del Cobre mine is still producing copper. By the beginning of the twentieth century, most of the copper in the mineshafts and tunnels had been removed, so in 1910 the Chino Copper Company, then owners of the mine, began open pit mining.

Under their guidance, Santa Rita was for a short time the largest open pit mine in the world.

After a succession of different owners, Santa Rita is owned today by the international mining company of Freeport-McMoRan, which operates copper, silver, and gold mines throughout the world. The small settlement of Santa Rita was long ago swallowed up by the huge open pit, which now measures more than a mile across and more than 1,300 feet deep.

Historians believe Mangas Coloradas was born around 1790 near Santa Lucia Springs, a tributary of the Gila River in the Mogollon Mountains a dozen miles west of what would become Santa Rita del Cobre. His homeland embraced the beautiful and extremely rugged region known today as the Gila Wilderness Area of the Gila National Forest.

One warm, clear day in the spring of 2019, I spent several hours on horseback exploring a small portion of the Gila, riding slowly through gently rolling countryside containing a mixed forest of juniper and cottonwoods. I was in the Arenas Valley, a natural corridor through this part of the Gila leading straight to Santa Rita. For a time, particularly after Pattie began managing Santa Rita, Mangas and the Apaches remained on friendly terms with the Americans and often visited and traded with them, likely riding the same route I was following.

I stopped at a rocky bluff overlooking a small creek where a pool of clear, greenish-blue spring water sparkled in the sun. Mangas and his followers almost certainly camped on the grassy, nearly flat opposite bank. As if on cue, three mule deer stepped out to graze in a small clearing in the trees as I stood there. Further back in the timber is a 400- to 500-year-old alligator juniper more than five feet in diameter and more than sixty feet tall, where Apaches met to plan their next moves.

The altitude there is around 6,000 feet, far below the higher peaks in the Gila that reach nearly 11,000 feet, but it was easy to see why the Apaches loved this area and resented any type of encroachment, whether from Spaniards, Mexicans, or

Americans. There are six different ecological zones here, ranging from Chihuahuan desert lowlands at just over 4,000 feet to the conifer forests of spruce and fir above 9,000 feet. It is that diversity that led to the designation of the Gila as the first official US Forest Service wilderness under the Wilderness Act passed by Congress in 1964.

By birth, Mangas Coloradas was a member of the Bedonkohe band, the smallest of the four Chiricahua bands, and he is believed to have been known among his people as Fuerte, the Spanish word for "strong." Even by his mid-twenties he stood well over six feet tall and weighed as much as two hundred pounds, unusually large for an Apache, which made him easily recognizable.

He married into the largest of the Apache bands, the Chihenne, and eventually one of his daughters, Dos-the-she, became a wife of Cochise of the Chokonen band. Mangas was the first Apache war chief to unite these three bands, as well as the fourth, the Nednhis, under single leadership, which he had done by 1840. Overall, however, the Chiricahua never numbered more than three thousand during his lifetime.

Mangas Coloradas certainly participated in the raids against Santa Rita del Cobre and northern Mexico, gaining leadership roles through these exploits. He was described as an organizer and careful planner who demonstrated intellect as well as bravery.

"Fuming bitterness and mutual disrespect finally burst forth in the spring of 1831, and relations between the two peoples were never the same after that," writes Edwin R. Sweeney in *Mangas Coloradas* (1998), his detailed biography of the great chief. "There was no large-scale uprising, nor was there a bloody massacre of a presidio or settlement. Instead, hostilities slowly gained momentum during the decade like a snowball increasing in size as it rolls downhill."

A week of attacks and raids killed fifty people in northern Chihuahua. In reprisal, troops from that state surprised an

Apache encampment on the Gila and reported killing twenty-two. To avenge these losses, during a six-month period between April and October 1833, Mangas and his war parties killed over two hundred in Sonora. Each action from one brought an equally violent reaction from the other.

Mistrust, treaties doomed to failure even before they were agreed to, and the October 1834 public execution by Sonoran military officials of an important Chiricahua chieftain and ally of Mangas Coloradas, Tutije, all fueled the fire. The following year, Sonora began offering bounties for Apache scalps, a hundred pesos for each Apache male over the age of fourteen. A few months later, Chihuahua began hiring mercenaries to hunt down Apaches.

In April 1837, one of those mercenaries, an American named John Johnson who lived in Sonora, headed north with a mixed band of Mexicans and Americans to see what he could collect. He found the Chiricahuas on April 20 and gained their confidence by feigning friendship and good will. The parties traded for two days, then on the morning of the third day Johnson and his men met the unsuspecting Apaches with a devastating round of cannon and musket fire, killing at least twenty.

Apache oral history records that Mangas Coloradas was present at the attack. At the first shot, he grabbed a baby and fled for safety. Only later did he realize the baby was his own son. Two of his four wives were killed at the scene, however. Mexican authorities had calculated that such an attack would bring the Chiricahuas to the peace table for good, but just the opposite occurred: the Apaches quickly sought revenge.

Among the first to feel their wrath was a party of twenty-two trappers, all of whom were slain, and it is said this was where Mangas Coloradas gained the name by which he is known to history. He reportedly tore the shirt off one of the slain men and donned it himself. The long sleeves were bright red, and from that time on he became known as Kan-da-zis-tlishishen, or Mangas Coloradas, "Red Sleeves."

This cycle of attack and retaliation between Sonora, Chihuahua, and the Apaches continued for the next several years. In June 1839, Chihuahuan authorities did what Sonora had done four years earlier and began paying a bounty on Apache scalps. One of the mercenaries they hired was well known to the Apaches, a man named James Kirker, who had been trading with them for years. He had been exchanging arms and ammunition for horses and mules the Chiricahua had captured during their raids.

An 1847 painting of Kirker by Thomas Martin Easterly shows a large man with an unsavory expression on his face. He is clean-shaven, but his long hair, parted on one side, covers both ears. His arms are folded, and while he wears a bowtie, the viewer comes away with the impression Kirker was not only a product of his time and place, but also an opportunist who would and did play on either side of the law, whichever was more beneficial.

Born in Killead, County Antrim, Ireland, in 1793, Kirker fled to the United States at the age of sixteen to avoid conscription into the Royal Navy. In 1822, he answered an advertisement in the *Missouri Republican* newspaper in St. Louis and joined William Henry Ashley's famous 1822 fur-trapping expedition up the Missouri. Among those with Kirker, helping pull and pole Ashley's keelboats upstream against the current, was another young adventurer whose name would over the next two decades become synonymous with the fur trade, Jim Bridger.

Kirker left the northern Rockies two years later and settled in New Mexico, where in 1826 he began working at the Santa Rita del Cobre mines. His job was to escort the copper-laden mule trains south to Chihuahua City. He was hired as a bounty hunter, since by 1835 he had become a Mexican citizen, and because he knew the Apaches.

The governor of Chihuahua, Jose Maria Irigoyen, even allowed the state militia to assist Kirker if he called for help in his bounty hunting. Male Apache scalps would bring 200 pesos, while women's and children's scalps were worth 150 pesos each. On Kirker's first outing, on December 26, 1839, he and his men attacked a small band of Apaches who had been soliciting peace in Janos, long a favorite Apache trading center in northern Chihuahua. Fifteen Apaches were killed and twenty more captured. His second attack came in April when he killed six men and captured thirteen women and children during a midnight raid on their camp.

Kirker's mercenary band was disbanded when the Apaches signed a peace agreement with Chihuahua in the spring of 1843. It was a tense time for both sides; the key to bringing both parties together at last was that Chihuahuan authorities included rations in the agreement. Mangas and his band honored the treaty for just over a year, until Sonoran troops followed the Apaches into Chihuahua and killed more than seventy-five of them in two days of vicious fighting.

That quickly, Chihuahua's chances for peace ended once again. As Apache raids increased from just ten in 1844 to more than two hundred in 1845, Kirker and his mercenaries were reorganized. On July 7, 1846, he and his scalp hunters killed more than 130 men, women, and children as they slept after a friendship party with plenty of alcohol thrown by the Mexicans in the village of Galeana. Mangas Coloradas and the rest of the Chiricahuas would never forget the slaughter.

For the next several years, northern Chihuahua and Sonora were literally under siege, not only by war parties led by Mangas, but by other younger chieftains and band leaders as well, including one named Cochise. Even as he was meeting with Stephen Watts Kearny and pledging his support to the American troops in October 1846, at the outbreak of the Mexican–American War, Mangas Coloradas was planning the first of several major retaliatory attacks on Mexico. By 1848, the Apaches had even forced one Sonoran settlement, Fronteras, which had been founded by the Spanish 250 years earlier, to be abandoned.

In an ironic turn of events, the Chihuahuan government, then bankrupt, could not afford to pay Kirker for his scalps, and instead offered him a commission in the Mexican army. He refused, and as war with the United States loomed on the horizon, he was forced to flee Mexico as an enemy of the state. A bounty was even placed on his head.

Kirker joined the American army, took part in the invasion of Mexico, and later guided gold miners to California in 1849. He died in that state in 1852.

It was the gold miners moving through his part of Apacheria in southwestern New Mexico that probably irritated Mangas Coloradas the most in the years immediately following the end of America's war with Mexico. Some were even mining in Santa Rita del Cobre, which had been closed since 1834. The parade never seemed to end, and Apache encounters with the emigrants became less and less friendly. On August 16, 1849, Apaches fought a battle near Santa Rita del Cobre with the First Dragoons and were forced to retreat into the mountains; a week later they ambushed an emigrant party and several Apaches were killed.

That meant a revenge attack, and so by the autumn of 1849, Mangas and the Chihenne found themselves facing a new enemy they had pledged to support just three years before. At the same time, he and his Chiricahua continued their fight against Sonora—a two-week-long retaliatory Apache raid earlier in January had killed ninety-eight and reportedly wounded many more—but with the Mexican War over, the Mexicans and Americans were now allies. The world of Mangas Coloradas had begun to shrink, and while he continued to try to accept the growing American presence, his distrust of the whites only grew.

Even when John Bartlett, who arrived at Santa Rita in May 1851 to survey the border between Mexico and the United States, assured Mangas his stay would be temporary, the Apache leader remained uneasy. He had every reason to be. Bartlett, as leader of the Boundary Commission, appointed by the secretary of the interior, brought with him some three hundred people, including not only his own survey staff but also that of his Mexican counterpart, along with a military escort of more than eighty troopers.

Bartlett, who before accepting the surveying assignment had held a variety of jobs back east and was perhaps as much as fifteen years younger than Mangas, got along well with the Apache chief. When he completed his work in August and moved to a different location, the leader of his military escort, Captain Louis Craig, suggested to his superior officer, Colonel Edwin Sumner, commander of the Department of New Mexico, that having troops stationed permanently at Santa Rita would help control the Apaches, since it would be right in the heart of their homeland. The War Department in Washington concurred, and a new fort, Fort Webster, was established there. A small portion of the wall of that original fort is still visible today along Main Street in Pinos Altos.

On January 23, 1852, when Mangas and his band approached Fort Webster to talk peace, they were instead fired upon. The Apaches responded by attacking the fort three days later, stealing a herd of cattle and in the process wounding several troopers. Colonel Sumner then responded with a month-long campaign against Mangas Coloradas, or any Apaches he could find.

He didn't find any, and the next time Mangas approached Sumner to talk about ending hostilities, the colonel agreed. They met on July 11 at Acoma Pueblo, a pueblo fortress constructed atop a steep-walled mesa south of present-day Grants, New Mexico. Acoma tribesmen fought a bloody three-day battle against the Spanish conquistadors there in January 1600, and visitors to Acoma today can climb the same rock steps Mangas Coloradas climbed to the summit. It was the only treaty he ever signed, which he did with a thumb print.

The treaty was ratified by Congress and signed by President Franklin Pierce on March 25, 1853, but at the same time, while Mangas agreed to stop his raids into Mexico, Congress failed to appropriate enough funds to subsidize the Apaches with food and clothing. Raids into Sonora, essentially to steal livestock to keep from starving, resumed; during three weeks of raiding in July 1853, Apaches killed more than 150 Sonorans. Mexican forces, using Apache scouts to track their brethren, fought back, often following the Apaches back into New Mexico.

Indian agents were assigned to work with the Indians, but few stayed very long, largely because of the continued shortage of promised rations. Finally, in May 1854, Dr. Michael Steck, who had been serving as the agent for the Jicarilla Apaches and Utes in northern New Mexico, was appointed to manage the Chiricahua. Fort Webster had been abandoned and then relocated along the Rio Grande near the present-day town of Hatch. It became known there as Fort Thorn, and this is where Steck set up his headquarters.

Mangas Coloradas, along with other Chiricahua chieftains, developed a strong respect for Steck, largely because he delivered the rations the government had promised. The raids into Mexico became less frequent as the Apaches became more dependent on the subsidy. Washington thought they could not only maintain peace with the Apaches with food and supplies but could also eventually make them self-sufficient. Thus, a large part of Steck's job became one of teaching the Apaches how to till the soil and plant different crops.

Steck's efforts were surprisingly successful, considering the Chiricahua had no experience as farmers. For decades their economy had been based on hunting wild game; gathering acorns, piñon nuts, berries, and mescal; and raiding into Mexico. Even Mangas began planting, but by 1857 with their rations, particularly corn and beef, beginning to decrease substantially, raiding began again. Mangas may not have even taken part in these raids, but early the next year, Sonoran troops caught a band of raiders and in the fighting two of his sons were killed.

Almost from his first day in office as the Chiricahua agent, Steck had recognized the need for a special Apache reservation, large enough to hold the Bedonkohes of Mangas Coloradas, the Chokonens of Cochise, and the Chihennes of then leader Delgadito. The reservation would include Santa Lucia Springs, the favorite haunt of Mangas Coloradas, located just west of Santa Rita, and also a portion of the Gila River valley, fertile land that would support farming.

In March 1860, Steck traveled to Washington to meet the Commissioner of Indian Affairs, who agreed to the reservation site. It would be approximately 225 square miles in size. Steck returned to New Mexico and in August met Mangas at Santa Lucia to begin laying out the new reservation, but he must have been appalled at what had happened to the area during his short absence.

On May 18, just about the time Steck had been negotiating in Washington, a prospector named Jacob Snively and his companions, who had simply stopped to get a drink of water in Bear Creek near Pinos Altos, discovered gold in the clear, shallow water. Within a month, gold fever had swept through the region and more than five hundred miners had invaded the Chihenne homeland. Within a year the town of Silver City was established. Although Mangas Coloradas had not taken part, other Apaches had responded the only way they understood: by attacking supply wagons and mule trains heading into the area.

These Americans were different from the ones Mangas Coloradas had encountered in previous years. The miners had no respect whatsoever for any Indians and openly challenged Steck for their right to the land. The agent, undoubtedly stunned and frustrated by the lack of government assistance in his attempts to remove the miners, decided to run for Congress in the October elections, and he won. Within a short time, he had left New Mexico for Washington.

At dawn on the morning of December 4, 1860, a group of perhaps two dozen miners attacked a band of Chihenne Chiricahua camped on the Mimbres River. This was the same band Cuchillo Negro had led until his death at the hands of

Colonel William Loring in May 1857. The miners killed four Apaches including a chieftain, wounded many more, captured much of their livestock, and took more than a dozen women and children hostage.

A week later, the Apache leader met with military officials. Both sides tried to defuse the situation, but at the same time Mangas demanded an explanation for the unprovoked attack. He received no satisfactory answers, for the miners had returned to their claims on Bear Creek as if nothing had happened. Mangas took his band westward to join Cochise and his Chokonen. Just two months later, on February 4, 1861, the Bascom Affair with Cochise occurred.

There is no question this misguided sequence of events contributed heavily in precipitating the bloody years of warfare that followed between the Apaches and all whites, military or civilian. In his after-action reports, Lieutenant Bascom reported Mangas Coloradas was present during the negotiations at his camp, although his exact role is unclear. What is clear is that Cochise unleashed a fury heretofore unseen by anyone in the Southwest in the preceding decades.

In his autobiography, *Geronimo*, edited by S. M. Barrett (2011), the famous warrior describes what followed in simple but elegant terms: "After all this trouble all of the Indians agreed not to be friendly with the white men any more. There was no general engagement, but a long struggle followed. The number killed in these troubles did not amount to much, but this treachery on the part of the soldiers had angered the Indians and revived memories of other wrongs, so that we never again trusted the United States troops."

Stein's Peak, Pinos Altos, the Mimbres River, Doubtful Canyon, Santa Rita del Cobre, Fort McLane, Fort Buchanan, Cooke's Peak, Dragoon Springs—the list of engagements over the next few months goes on and on. Americans, Mexicans, miners, ranchers, farmers, former Butterfield employees, freighters, stockmen, and army troops all became Apache targets.

Mangas Coloradas, now some seventy years old, took an active role, even though Cochise, his son-in-law, largely directed the planning and the attacks.

Victorio, who was now leader of the Warm Springs band and had also advocated peace, began to take an active role in the fighting. Their combined goal, their mission, was to drive the whites—all of them—out of Apacheria. In Cooke's Canyon alone, a narrow canyon that also offered dependable water, the Apaches are said to have ambushed and killed more than a hundred whites between 1861 and 1863.

For a time, Mangas Coloradas and Cochise actually thought they were doing just that, as first the Butterfield stage ceased operation through Apache land and then one military fort after another was abandoned. Neither of the two great chieftains ever truly understood the real reason: the outbreak of the Civil War that pulled American soldiers back to battlefields in the East.

In the spring of 1862, the Apaches encountered another foe, a force of 2,350 largely volunteer troops known as the California Column. Led by Brigadier General James H. Carleton, they had been ordered east to stop the Confederate invasion of Arizona and New Mexico. Unknown to Carleton at the time, the Confederates, led by General Henry H. Sibley, had already been pushed out of the region.

That left Carleton largely free to fight the Apaches, which a detachment of his troops did on July 15 at Apache Pass. Cochise, Mangas Coloradas, and likely Victorio watched as the soldiers entered the seven-mile pass, a low divide separating the Chiricahua Mountains from the smaller Dos Cabezas range south of the present-day city of Wilcox. The Pass had a permanent spring, the first available water in forty miles when coming from Tucson, as well as plenty of grass for grazing horses or cattle.

The Apaches began firing sometime around late morning, according to various reports, and Cochise has been quoted as believing his men could kill every one of the soldiers. What they did not know was that this detachment of approximately 126 men had brought with them two howitzers, which both the troopers and Apaches later agreed swung the fighting in favor of the Americans.

Of more importance, perhaps, was the fact Mangas Coloradas was severely wounded in the fighting. Most believe the shot was fired by Private John Teal, who had become separated from his comrades and was pursued by some forty to fifty Apaches. One particular Apache began firing at Teal, who was trying to find any type of cover available. He continued firing back at the Indian, who had taken cover behind some bushes, and one of his shots connected. Teal later learned he had been in a duel with Mangas Coloradas, who was quickly carried off by other warriors.

Mangas was taken into Mexico to the Apache-friendly town of Janos, where a doctor removed the bullet and he recovered. He returned to his longtime hideouts in the Mogollon Mountains of New Mexico, but his fighting days and his war alliance with his son-in-law had ended. In September, he traveled again to the Pueblo at Acoma, where he had signed the treaty with Colonel Edwin Sumner more than a decade earlier, to ask them to approach the Americans about peace. Neither Carleton nor his associate, Brigadier General Joseph Rodman West, who had been with Carleton at Apache Pass and who now commanded troops in the District of Arizona, were interested.

Carleton hated the Apaches, as did West, and blamed all the atrocities of the recent past specifically on Mangas Coloradas. The two officers planned a military campaign against him, to be centered in and around Pinos Altos. Simultaneously, in early January 1863, Mangas led half his band to the old mining settlement to seek peace as well as a handout of rations. Some soldiers there agreed to issue food and supplies if Mangas would return in two weeks with his band.

Victorio, Nana, and Geronimo argued with him not to go, but it was at last decided Mangas would go back with half of his followers. That way, at least if there was treachery, the others would still be safe.

An American acquaintance of Mangas at Pinos Altos, Jack Swilling, who had helped convince Mangas to come back, met the old chief as he came in. Daniel Ellis Conner, a twenty-five-year-old Kentuckian and a member of Swilling's party, wrote later in his book, *Joseph Reddeford Walker and the Arizona Adventure*, that Mangas was "a large athletic man considerably over six feet in height . . . His shoulders were broad and his chest full, and muscular. He stood erect and his step was proud and altogether he presented quite a model of physical manhood."

Swilling, however, had turned as treacherous as Carleton and West. With gunmen hidden around the camp, he took Mangas prisoner and the next day took him to the abandoned Fort McLane where General West was waiting. "The Gen. [West] walked out to where Mangas was in custody to see him and looked like a pygmy beside the old Chief, who also towered above everybody about him in stature," continues Conner. They did not bind or shackle Mangas, but put him in an open room with a constant guard.

What occurred next has been recorded by two different witnesses at Fort McLane, Daniel Conner and Private Clark Stocking of Company A, Fifth California Infantry. Both accounts are widely accepted by historians, even though each contradicts the official report given by General West.

West met with his guards the night of January 18 and gave them their instructions. His exact words, according to Stocking, who was present and is believed to have been one of the guards, were as follows: "Men, that old murderer has got away from every soldier command and has left a trail of blood for 500 miles on the old stage line. I want him dead or alive tomorrow morning, do you understand? I want him dead."

Conner was a member of Joseph Walker's party of prospectors who had been camped at the abandoned fort and who shared night guard duty with West's troops after they arrived.

He was on guard duty that night and was present when new military guards came on duty at midnight and began to taunt Mangas. He noticed that whenever he moved a few steps into the darkness where the guards could not see him, that the old chieftain began acting restless. His erratic movements, Conner realized, were in response to the hot bayonets the guards were touching to his feet.

Around 1:00 a.m., as Conner saw the chief lift himself on his left elbow and angrily tell the soldiers to stop, the two guards immediately shot him at point-blank range. Stocking has added that Sergeant Henry Foljaine, a third guard that night, then rushed in and shot Mangas in the back of the head with a pistol. West, by dramatic contrast, filled his official report on January 23, 1863, with statements describing how, within an hour, Mangas had made "three efforts to escape and was shot on the third attempt." That report has since been completely dismissed by serious historians.

According to Sweeney and others, the following morning the body was simply thrown into a ditch and covered with dirt and rocks, but several days later some of the soldiers, along with David B. Sturgeon, a military surgeon with West's troops, unearthed the body and severed the head. They reportedly boiled the head in a kettle of water to help preserve it, and Sturgeon later took the skull with him to Ohio where he gave it to a phrenologist named Orson S. Fowler. Fowler described the skull as one of the largest he had ever seen.

For most people, that is where the story ends, but it may not really be the end of the story. Several years ago, an old man in Deming told a story about an experience he had had when he was five years old. He and his father were up on a ridge not far from the site of the old fort where his father was digging a hole with his shovel. Not very far down in the soft, sandy soil, they uncovered a skeleton, the man related.

They could tell it was the skeleton of a very large man, and that the skull was missing. They felt sure it was Mangas

Coloradas, and they carefully reburied the skeleton. After that, they never went back to the site.

Those who have heard this story and know the area are pretty sure the man's story has validity. They believe the Apaches went to the fort where Mangas was killed, dug up his body, and reburied it after all the soldiers left, a not uncommon occurrence.

Carleton and West believed by killing Mangas Coloradas that the remaining Chiricahua would surrender peacefully, accept their fate, and the two of them would receive credit for ending the American war with the Apaches. Such idealistic thinking showed just how little the Americans in general, and

This historical marker on US Highway 80 south of the town of Hurley marks the approximate location of where Mangas Coloradas was murdered at Fort McLane. Nothing remains of the fort itself, which was abandoned in 1861.

the United States Army in particular, understood the foe they were fighting.

"Mangas Coloradas had been the single most influential Apache leader throughout the 1850s," writes William S. Kiser in *Dragoons in Apacheland* (2012), "and countless times he had expressed his good will toward the Anglo-Americans. Virtually every Indian agent and Army officer in the territory had become acquainted with him, so great was his importance."

Instead of bringing the Apaches crawling to the peace table, the murder of Mangas Coloradas had exactly the opposite effect, for it added another act of treachery to the long list of broken trusts by the Americans. This one was worse because the chieftain had been shot not in battle, but rather within a few hours after he had come unarmed into the white camp to seek peace. The mutilation of his body added further insult. Mangas Coloradas had, in actuality, only waged war against the Americans for two years.

CHAPTER 5

THE AMERICANS: BRIGADIER GENERAL JOSEPH R. WEST

Brigadier General Joseph Rodman West, despite serving in both the Mexican War and the American Civil War and later as a United States senator from Louisiana, is remembered more for his giant ego and for his treachery in ordering the murder of Mangas Coloradas after the chieftain had come in under a flag of truce to discuss peace terms. West's official report of Mangas's death—that he was shot while trying to escape—has been universally discredited. The manner in which Mangas was killed and his body later mutilated created a lasting mistrust of Americans by the Apaches and contributed to another quarter century of warfare.

West was born on September 19, 1822 in New Orleans, but two years later his parents moved to Philadelphia, where he attended private schools and later studied at the University of Pennsylvania. By 1841, however, he had returned to New Orleans. In 1847, as the war with Mexico intensified, he enlisted and served as a captain of mounted cavalry in an independent company attached to the Regiment of Maryland and District of Columbia Volunteers.

At the conclusion of the war West moved to California, where he became interested in newspaper work and soon became the owner of a paper in San Francisco. He was still in California when the Civil War broke out in April 1861, and that August he entered the Union Army as a lieutenant colonel in the First California Volunteer Infantry Regiment commanded by Colonel James H. Carleton. West was thus united with one of the most notorious Indian-haters in the West, and historians have since wondered if this association, combined with his strong ego, led to West's own anti-Apache feelings.

In late 1861 and into early 1862, Confederate General Henry H. Sibley's volunteer force invaded New Mexico and on March 20–21 defeated Union soldiers in the Battle of Valverde, a crossing on the Rio Grande south of present-day Socorro. From there, Sibley marched his Army of New Mexico, as he himself named it, northward where he captured both Albuquerque and Santa Fe. On March 28, however, after his supply train was destroyed at the Battle of Glorieta Pass east of Santa Fe, he was forced to retreat back into Texas. This ended the Confederate invasion of the Southwest.

Carleton did not know this, and in April he began leading some 2,350 men eastward from Drum Barracks in Wilmington, California, toward the Rio Grande to drive out the Confederates. This became known as the California Column, and in addition to West and the First California Volunteer Infantry also included volunteer cavalry and artillery companies.

The California Column followed the route of the Butterfield Overland Mail, which had been discontinued in 1860, and they traveled largely by foot in groups of about four hundred men, in order to preserve water along the way. En route, Carleton was promoted to brigadier general. On May 20, 1862, West and the first troops of the California Column entered and took control of Tucson, and by the first week of June, the majority of the Column had arrived.

When Carleton learned the Confederate threat no longer existed, he turned his full attention to subduing the Apaches, and one of his first orders of business was to send two companies of his First California Cavalry (about 140 men) out to scout the remaining two-hundred-plus miles to the Mesilla Valley and the Rio Grande. From Tucson, the route to the Rio Grande led through a seven-mile break in the mountains known as Apache Pass, which contained the only reliable spring water in the area. On June 25, this advance force was stopped by Cochise as it approached the spring. After several hours of negotiating, the chief allowed the men to pass through.

On July 9, West, who by now had been promoted to full colonel, ordered 126 of his men under the command of Captain Thomas L. Roberts to move through Apache Pass and on to the Rio Grande. To his credit, West ordered Roberts to avoid any confrontation with the Apaches unless the Indians became the aggressors. Just in case this happened, West made certain Roberts took along two howitzers.

Roberts and sixty-eight soldiers (he had divided his command earlier) arrived at the pass sometime between 10:00 a.m. and noon on July 15, where Cochise, Mangas Coloradas, Juh, Victorio, and others were waiting for them. In her memorable book, *Indeh* (1980), author Eve Ball quotes Daklugie, the son of Juh, who describes what has since become known as the Battle of Apache Pass: "Juh believed that they could easily have defeated the White Eyes had they not used terrible weapons new to the Indians: huge guns mounted on wheels.

"The Army officers reported later that they had killed many Apaches, but the Indians who participated in that battle denied this. The Apaches realized that they could not compete with the cannon, so they withdrew without losing a man. Most of the Indians were armed only with bows and arrows."

A week later, Carleton, West, and their men moved safely through Apache Pass without incident, probably unaware Mangas Coloradas had been seriously wounded in the battle and certainly unaware that the chieftain had realized his fighting days were over. Nonetheless, Carleton ordered the construction of Fort Bowie in Apache Pass to protect the route and the water for Americans. Construction began on July 28, less than two

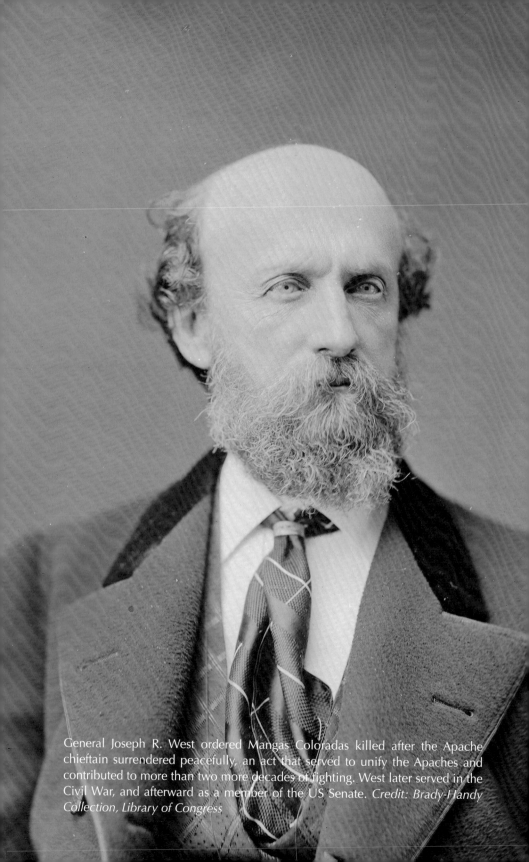

General Joseph R. West ordered Mangas Coloradas killed after the Apache chieftain surrendered peacefully, an act that served to unify the Apaches and contributed to more than two more decades of fighting. West later served in the Civil War, and afterward as a member of the US Senate. *Credit: Brady-Handy Collection, Library of Congress*

weeks after the battle. Carleton continued to Santa Fe, where he took command of the Department of New Mexico. Reports of Apache raiding arrived continuously, and because Carleton had seen the results of such raiding after leaving Apache Pass— including dead bodies and burned wagons—his attitude toward the Apaches became more extreme.

In October 1862, he ordered his men to reject any and all flags of truce and to kill all male Indians capable of bearing arms. West, promoted to brigadier general, apparently accepted Carleton's order without question, and when Mangas Coloradas came in to Fort McLane under a flag of truce to seek peace in January 1863, West ordered his execution.

Barely a month later, West established a fort on the east side of Gila River and named it after himself (it was abandoned less than a year later). By summer, as the Chokonens, Bedonkohes, and Chihennes joined forces to avenge Mangas's death, their brutality seemed to surprise even West, who, despite what he had already seen, apparently did not believe the Chiricahuas could organize themselves well enough to mount any type of unified offensive.

On June 17, an army lieutenant and two others were killed while crossing the Rio Grande. The officer's head had been cut off and his chest ripped open, almost certainly to remind West of how the body of Mangas Coloradas had been muti- lated. The act infuriated West and he ordered the commander of Fort West, Captain William McCleave, to begin pursuing the Apaches immediately and to kill any and all he found. Many attacks by the Apaches took place in Cooke's Canyon and around Cooke's Peak, a travel route west of the present-day town of Hatch, New Mexico. West made a special trip to the canyon to emphasize his orders to the captain. He and Carleton also ordered the establishment of Fort Cummings on a low ridge overlooking the canyon.

The following April, as the Civil War continued to grind on, West was ordered to Arkansas, where he was given command of the Second Division of VII Corps. It was the last the Apaches would see of West, but his actions have never been forgotten. The unit fought in the Red River Campaign, a series of battles in south Louisiana initiated by the Union and designed to take control of the river, capture Shreveport, and occupy east Texas. The campaign was a failure, and some believe may have extended the war by several months, as it diverted Union troops from a larger objective, the port city of Mobile, which was not captured until the following year.

West later led the First Division of Cavalry in the Military Division of the Southwest, taking the division from Shreveport to San Antonio, where he was active in Reconstruction efforts until January 4, 1866, when he was mustered out of the army as a brevetted major general. He returned to New Orleans and served as a deputy United States Marshal until 1871, when he was elected to the US Senate. He served until 1877 but did not run for reelection. West was a member of the Board of Commissioners of the District of Columbia from 1882 until 1885, and was president of the board, the same office as a mayor today, in 1882 and 1883.

He died in Washington on October 31, 1898, and is buried in Arlington National Cemetery.

CHAPTER 6

PLACES TO SEE: SANTA RITA DEL COBRE, PINOS ALTOS

The historical marker honoring Mangas Coloradas, located on the east side of US Highway 180 one mile south of the Grant County Airport and four miles south of the town of Hurley, marks the approximate location where Fort McLane once stood. Never more than a small collection of log buildings, today nothing remains of the fort where Mangas Coloradas was killed.

Originally named Fort Floyd but later renamed Fort McLane, the small garrison was established on October 9, 1860. Its primary purpose was to provide protection for the mining operations in Pinos Altos and Santa Rita, but the fort was abandoned in the summer of 1861 when troops were transferred to Fort Fillmore near Mesilla.

The original Santa Rita del Cobre copper mine was located a short distance from Fort McLane; today the wall from the discarded tailings is visible for miles. According to oral history, an Apache took Lieutenant Colonel Jose Manuel Carrasco to the secret valley where copper was clearly visible on the ground, and the area continues to be an active copper mine today. After a succession of different owners, it is currently owned by the international mining company of Freeport-McMoRan, which operates copper, silver, and gold mines throughout the world.

Open pit mining began in 1910 and soon swallowed up the settlement of Santa Rita, where at one time as many as 6,000 residents lived. The open pit now measures nearly two miles across and more than 1,300 feet deep, making it one of the largest in the world.

The mine is approximately twelve miles east of Silver City. A high fence blocks visitors from the immediate work area, but a parking pull-off along New Mexico Highway 152 provides partial views of the open pit and shows the scale of the operation today.

Pinos Altos is six miles north of Silver City on New Mexico Highway 15. Upon entering the town, turn left to follow the

Originally just a small valley where copper literally lay on the surface, today the Santa Rita del Cobre mine is owned by the international mining company Freeport-McMoRan and has become one of the largest open pit mines in the world, producing not only copper but also silver and gold.

The open pit mine is now nearly two miles across and more than 1,300 feet deep, and the mountain of tailings is visible for miles.

All that remains of the original Fort Webster in Pinos Altos is this entrance, which today leads to a private home. Established in January 1852, Fort Webster was the scene of continuing confrontations with the Apaches until it was abandoned in September 1852, and relocated fourteen miles east on the Mimbres River.

Historic Loop, which leads to the Buckhorn Saloon and the Opera House, where dinner is served each night except Sunday (reservations required). Across the street from the Buckhorn is an 1866 log cabin that served as the first school in Grant County. Less than a mile from the school, the road crosses Bear Creek, where gold was discovered in 1860, which led to the establishment of Silver City.

CHAPTER 7

THE APACHES: COCHISE

To the Mexicans, the Americans, and the Apaches, the village was known as Galeana. It was, and still is, located along the Rio Santa Maria in Chihuahua, about fifty miles east of the border with Sonora and a little over a hundred miles due south of the New Mexico state line. It was one of many such settlements the Apaches visited and occasionally raided, and with the exception of a few brief hours of horror just after dawn on the morning of July 7, 1846, Galeana might have faded into history like so many other similar Chihuahuan and Sonoran towns.

That morning, bounty hunter James Kirker and his band of volunteers, including some from Galeana itself, murdered some 130 (other estimates put the number killed closer to 150) Chiricahua Apaches while they slept. Kirker, already well known to the Apaches because of his bounty hunting attacks nearly a decade earlier, had invited the Indians to Galeana to have a feast and to talk peace. Despite serious misgivings, the Apaches had agreed. As evening fell, mescal was flowing freely; the next morning, while the Indians slept off their celebration, Kirker and his men walked quietly among them, smashing their heads with clubs. Then they scalped them.

Among those slain were a number of important Chiricahua leaders, including two men named Relles and Pisago Cabezon. One of these may have been the father of another Apache who

No known photographs of Cochise exist, but he is said to have resembled his younger son Naiche, shown here with his wife. Cochise was described by one who knew him, "as fine a looking Indian as one ever saw." *Credit: Ben Wittick Collection, Palace of the Governors Photo Archives, New Mexico Historical Museum*

would, through his vengeance, rise to become the greatest chieftain the Chiricahua would ever have, a warrior named Cochise. Whether or not Relles or Pisago Cabezon was the father of Cochise will likely never be known for certain, according to Freddie Kay-dah-zinne, the great-great-grandson of Cochise.

"Apache history is complicated and difficult for non-Apaches to understand," explained Kay-dah-zinne during one of our visits in the Cultural Center on the Mescalero Reservation, "because in our language, names are usually too difficult for historians to write, so they use the names the Spanish created. We only know these people by their Apache names, so sometimes we don't know who they're talking about. Also, many of our people have never talked to writers or historians about certain individuals or things that may have happened to them, so that creates a gap in the history, too.

"We do know that in those days a lot of leadership was inherited. If your father was a leader, it was often handed down to you. Relles and Pisago Cabezon are Mexican names of two who probably were leaders, and it is certainly possible one may have been Cochise's father, my great-great-great-grandfather."

Jason Betzinez, a cousin of Geronimo, described Galeana on the very first page of his book *I Fought with Geronimo* (1959) as "the bloodiest conflict in which Apaches were ever involved." For Cochise, the treachery at Galeana affected his relationships not only with Mexicans but also with Americans for the rest of his life. The Indians had come into Chihuahua seeking peace, but in just two hours Kirker and his men changed the course of history. Today the Apaches use the word *ka na ji ch aa* to describe what happened that fateful morning. It means "trail of trust," or "disloyalty."

Kay-dah-zinne did agree with historians who have described Galeana as one of several life-changing events for Cochise, even though the Apache leader was not present at the massacre. Cochise was then around forty, and at the time of his birth, probably between 1800 and 1810, the Apaches, Mexicans, and

Spaniards were living in relative peace. After decades of fighting the Apaches, the Spaniards realized they could never defeat them militarily and changed their strategy to one of pacification through trade and support. Food and supplies were handed out at different presidios across northern Mexico, and Apache bands were encouraged to settle near them. Several bands did move and began living peacefully near presidios at Janos in Chihuahua and Fronteras in Sonora.

Presidios were in effect small military bases, and between the mid-1500s and mid-1800s, the Spanish constructed more than two hundred of them through a colonial empire that stretched across North Africa, Central America, and Mexico. San Diego, Santa Fe, and Tucson, among other modern-day American cities, each served as a presidio. The word "presidio" has two meanings, garrison and prison, so even while many presidios established prior to 1750 were not fortified, every one had a guardhouse.

Those not constructed with a protective wall around them were simply clusters of small buildings that housed fifty to sixty poorly trained militia, who attempted to protect the frontier while at the same time advancing the Spanish culture. The militia was made up of settlers, farmers, miners, and other colonists who had virtually no experience—or success—in fighting the Apaches.

Recognizing this ineffectiveness, in 1786 Spain began to change its presidio policy. New presidios were created and others relocated to form a line of fortresses stretching from the Gulf of Mexico westward to the Gulf of California along what is essentially the United States-Mexico border today. Each of the presidios was built with four adobe outer walls measuring approximately 550 feet long, ten to fourteen feet tall, and two to four feet thick. Guard towers were constructed on the corners, and the interior buildings included quarters for the presidio *capitan* and his officers, a chapel, and the guardhouse. The walls of these interior buildings were nearly a foot thick.

There were slight variations in the construction, but, writes Jack Williams in his essay, *The Evolution of the Presidio in Northern New Spain* (2004), the Spanish quickly realized that even these new "modernized" fortifications had not improved the effectiveness of the army in their war against the Indians.

In 1810, Mexico's war of independence from Spain began, and it continued until 1821. The decade-long struggle siphoned both funds and personnel from the presidios along the northern frontier, resulting in a continual shortage of arms, supplies, and payments to troops who remained in them. Rations to the Apaches living near those presidios were also cut drastically, and as a result, they began subsistence raiding again. The presidio system continued to decline in the years immediately following the end of the revolution because the now independent Mexican government had no funds to sustain them, and as Apache discontent grew, both Chihuahua and Sonora became battlegrounds once again.

The Apaches reestablished themselves in their ancestral homelands of Arizona and New Mexico, often bringing their stolen Mexican horses and cattle to Santa Rita del Cobre, where they exchanged them illegally to white traders for other supplies, particularly arms and ammunition. Without question, Cochise took part in these raids, and as the fighting became more intense during the next few years, his name became known to the Mexicans, who, according to old records, spelled it "Chees." Mexican forces, frustrated by their inability to defend their ranches and settlements, began to take the offensive and invade Apacheria.

The Apaches responded with more and fiercer raids and attacks, and because there were losses on both sides, the fighting turned into a war of retaliation. In 1835, Sonora authorized a bounty for the scalp of any Apache male over the age of fourteen, and soon after, Chihuahua began hiring mercenaries to hunt down the Apaches. An early morning surprise attack on April 22, 1837, by a group of those mercenaries, led by an American named John Johnson, left twenty Chiricahua dead in southwestern New Mexico. In an eerie foreshadowing of the same type of trickery James Kirker would use nine years later at Galeana, Johnson and his men opened fire after two days of peaceful trading with the Apaches.

The fighting continued like this year after year, which, despite the Mexican treachery, is why Relles and Pisago Cabezon and their followers traveled southward to Chihuahua in the summer of 1846 in hopes of securing a peace. They were tired of war, and when James Kirker invited them to Galeana to talk peace, they were suspicious but still willing to go.

What the Mexicans failed to understand was that these types of treachery were not forgotten by the Apaches. They responded with increased fury, in which, as Sweeney describes so well in his biography of Cochise, revenge and plunder became dual objectives. They did not stop after a single attack, or even after a year of war party attacks on multiple targets ranging from individuals to ranches to entire towns, and it mattered not who the victims were. Literally, generations of Apaches took up the fight.

That is what took Cochise back to Fronteras in June 1848. Driving their stolen cattle and horses taken in a recent raid near the town, the Apaches were ambushed by the Sonorans and two warriors were killed. The next day, Cochise and his men skirmished with the Sonorans again, and somehow Cochise was captured. Accounts of the incident are sketchy, but the captured Apache's name was recorded by the Mexicans as "Cucchisle," which leaves little doubt it was Cochise. He was shackled and led to either a vacant building or possibly to a small cave where he was imprisoned. Either would have been cramped and dirty, and escape was virtually impossible.

Apache oral history does not include this specific event, but it is known the Mexicans did capture one Apache during the fighting and that he was put in irons. It is almost certain he was not locked in the presidio guardhouse, because seven Mexicans were already being held there. It is also known that the followers of Cochise immediately laid siege to Fronteras, setting up their camp within five miles of the undermanned presidio. Then they moved to within a mile of the town.

No supplies could come in and no one could get out to bring back reinforcements. For certain, wherever he was held, any meals Cochise received were given grudgingly because everyone else was nearly starving. In August when a party of twenty-three soldiers and citizens attempted to break through the cordon to get desperately needed food, the Apaches killed or captured all but one of them. Finally, on August 11, some six weeks after Cochise had been captured, the presidio commander, Captain Calvo y Muro, ransomed him back to the Apaches in exchange for five soldiers and six civilians captured during the siege. Not long afterward, the Fronteras presidio, built in 1692 and the oldest in Sonora, was abandoned because of the damage the Apache siege had caused.

Cochise was not the undisputed leader of the Chiricahua Apaches at the time of his capture, but rather a sub-chief. By then he was gathering his own followers as he distinguished himself in different attacks against the Mexicans, but he himself was still following his father-in-law, Mangas Coloradas, and his band leader, Miguel Narbona. Now, it seemed, they were avenging not only Galeana, but also the imprisonment of Cochise. In December, the Apaches struck Tubac, another presidio not far from Tucson. They killed nine people and spread such fear among the remaining inhabitants that Tubac, like Fronteras just a few months earlier, was abandoned.

The end of the Mexican–American War in 1848 not only resulted in the transfer of much of Apacheria into US control but also increased American activity in the region. By 1850, the inevitable clashes and skirmishes between the Apaches and these newcomers had already started. To make matters worse, at least for the Apaches, the different bands were split on the issue of establishing peace with Sonora, which some thought could offer them a safe haven from the Americans.

Mangas Coloradas, Miguel Narbona, and Cochise were opposed to any conditions of peace, undoubtedly remembering the treachery at Galeana and fearful of another such attack. They continued their raiding, often targeting the Sonoran village and presidio of Bacoachi, reportedly with the intention of forcing its abandonment, as with Fronteras and Tubac. For the year 1850, Sweeney puts the total number of Sonorans killed during these raids at 111, but it likely was higher. The number increased to more than 200 the next year.

Following his six weeks of captivity at Fronteras, little, if any, pure evidence of Cochise's personal involvement in any of these fights has been recorded, although historians virtually all agree he did take an active role in them. By Apache custom and tradition, he would have felt an inherited hatred for the Mexicans, amplified by the murders committed by Johnson and Kirker that time would never dim. He was physically in his prime, standing nearly six feet tall, slim and muscular, and because his father had been an Apache leader, Cochise certainly accepted his role as a future leader.

"Our people called him Cheis, which is sometimes interpreted as 'oak,'" writes historian Eve Ball in *Indeh,* quoting Daklugie, the son of Juh, a childhood friend of Cochise. "In a sense it does mean that, though it indicates the strength and quality of oak rather than the wood itself. Who added the prefix I do not know—perhaps some military officer. Our language is a difficult one, and it is not strange that mistakes have been made."

"My relatives told me he was a very handsome man who looked more like his son Naiche than his oldest son Taza," said Kay-dah-zinne. "He was well respected. When he would ride into camp on his horse, there was some sort of spiritual aura about him. People could feel that this man had a special power, some kind of special gifts. When somebody is like Cochise, we think of them as receiving a special gift from God, and that they themselves were a gift to us."

James Henry Tevis, who came to know Cochise several years later while managing the Butterfield stage station at Apache

Pass, described the Chiricahua leader in his book *Arizona in the 50s* (1954): "as fine a looking Indian as one ever saw. He was about six feet tall and as straight as an arrow, built from the ground up, as perfect as any man could be."

Cochise emerged as the leader of the Chokonen Chiricahua upon the death of Miguel Narbona sometime in the mid-1850s. Despite his Spanish name, Narbona was a Chiricahua. He had been captured as a young boy by the Mexican military and adopted by the family of Captain Antonio Narbona, with whom he remained for about ten years. He was sent to a Christian school and kept his Spanish name, even after he escaped and returned to his Apache band. During his years of servitude, however, he had developed an undying hatred for the Mexicans. This hatred, as well as his skill and daring in fighting them, undoubtedly influenced his understudy, Cochise, during their years together.

Something else also occurred early in the decade that affected Mexican, American, and Apache relationships in the months and years to come. The Gadsden Treaty, in which Mexico sold additional land to the United States—Apacheria, in effect—was ratified by Congress on April 25, 1854. The treaty essentially established the present US–Mexico boundary, and under the terms of the treaty, Mexican forces were not allowed to cross that boundary into the United States. Cochise and his Chokonens, living in Apache Pass and in the Chiricahua and Dragoon Mountains of southern Arizona, learned this and used it to their advantage for several years until the next wave of Americans made their presence known.

Initially, Cochise wanted peace with the Americans, and he tried to avoid any major encounters with them. This became more and more difficult, especially after the Butterfield Overland Mail Company built one of its stations in Apache Pass in July 1858 and their coaches began making twice-weekly trips through the pass, less than a mile from where he and his band usually camped.

The Apaches continued to raid into Sonora and Chihuahua, but as more Americans moved into their homelands, they also realized that simultaneously fighting the Mexicans and the American encroachment would leave them no safe haven. Thus, that summer Cochise decided to solicit peace with Sonora.

On July 14, 1858, they came to Fronteras to negotiate, and once again the Mexicans resorted to treachery. After they had gotten the Apaches drunk, Mexican forces apparently opened fire on them, not only in the reopened presidio but also literally in the streets of the village. Some reports say the Apaches started the incident when a soldier was killed by a drunk Indian, but regardless, by the time it was over, thirty-six Apache men and women had been killed.

Again, neither Cochise nor Mangas Coloradas were present, but the two joined forces later in the summer of 1858 and on September 16 staged a retaliatory attack on Fronteras. The attack failed, largely due to cannon fire from the presidio, but Cochise and his band spent the rest of the month raiding through Sonora in revenge before returning to Apache Pass. By November the Apaches were ready to raid Fronteras again, but Mexican patrols intercepted them and once more drove them back into Arizona.

These events led Cochise to think instead that it might be more advantageous to make peace with the Americans instead of the Mexicans. There are many reports that Cochise and his band even entered into an agreement with the Americans to supply the Butterfield station in Apache Pass with firewood, and although there apparently was never an actual written contract for this, most, including Kay-dah-zinne, feel certain it is true. Cochise and his warriors could have easily wiped out the station, but chose not to. Additionally, numerous travelers going through Apache Pass on the stage line described seeing Apaches standing peacefully around the station, and firewood was never in short supply.

Apache Pass was one of the 141 stations built by John W. Butterfield and his associates after they had won the United

States government's contract to deliver mail between St. Louis and San Francisco on March 3, 1857. Prior to Butterfield's contract for overland delivery, mail bound for California had to be taken by ship to Panama, carried by mules across the isthmus to the Pacific, then transported again by ship up the Pacific coast to California. Butterfield's contract was for $600,000, and on September 16, 1858, personally carrying two mailbags, he left St. Louis on the maiden run.

His small stations, generally made of rock or adobe with room for two to four employees as well as fresh horses, were located an average of about twenty miles apart at reliable water sources along the entire 2,795-mile route. To the east, Butterfield also built a station at Doubtful Canyon along what would become the New Mexico-Arizona border, and another west of Apache Pass at Dragoon Springs. In the years to come, Cochise and his warriors would attack all three.

In December 1858, Cochise and his band were doing their best to live peacefully with the Americans. That month, he is believed to have had his first-ever direct encounter with an American. That man was Dr. Michael Steck, who in 1853 had been appointed as the temporary Indian agent for the Chiricahua. The following April, during another visit to Apache Pass, Steck issued rations and supplies to Cochise and his band.

Cochise gave his word to the agent he would continue to watch over the interests of the station and even protect travelers coming through Apache Pass, but several months later, when three Apaches were killed after raiding a ranch for horses and cattle, his mood toward the Americans apparently changed to one of distrust. He and his men were blamed for stealing horses from the Dragoon Springs station during the fall of 1860, an incident that increased American distrust of Cochise. Once again history was repeating itself, only this time the Apache leader was caught between two totally different cultures, and the Apaches' own culture did not mesh with either one.

This is all that remains of the Butterfield Stage station in Apache Pass where Cochise met Lt. George Bascom. Some of the fighting between Bascom and the Apaches took place in the open ground around the station as well as in the station itself.

The match that lit the fuse that set off open, continuous warfare between Cochise and the Americans was struck on January 27, 1861. That day, Pinal Apaches attacked John Ward's ranch in the Sonoita Valley of southern Arizona. Some twenty head of cattle were stolen, and Ward's twelve-year-old son Felix was taken hostage. Ward himself was not present, but neighbors sent a message to Fort Buchanan eleven miles away, and Second Lieutenant George N. Bascom was assigned by Buchanan's commanding officer, Colonel Pitcairn Morrison, to follow the Indian trail until the boy and cattle were recovered. The young lieutenant was further authorized by Morrison to use force, if necessary, to recover the boy.

Because Morrison and Bascom had only been in Arizona a few months, neither was familiar with the raiding habits of Cochise or the Chiricahuas. If they had been, they would have known Cochise rarely if ever took captives. Thus, Morrison might have reasoned the raid on the Ward ranch had been done by a different band, but he didn't. Believing the trail led to Apache Pass, Bascom, John Ward, and fifty-four men of the Seventh Infantry headed that way, arriving on the afternoon of February 3. Before reaching the stage station, they met Sergeant Daniel Robinson and thirteen troopers just returning from Fort McLane, located not far from Pinos Altos and the Santa Rita mines. Robinson and his men joined Bascom's detail and remained with him until the lieutenant returned to Fort Buchanan.

At the stage station, Bascom met James Wallace and Charles Culver, Butterfield employees who both knew Cochise. Word was sent to the Apache chieftain to come in for talks, which he did later the following day. With Cochise came his wife and two of his young children, one of whom may have been Naiche, his second son; his brother Coyuntura; and three other relatives. By bringing his family with him, one has to believe Cochise felt no fear or mistrust of Bascom when the lieutenant invited him and Coyuntura into his tent to eat. Ward joined them, possibly acting as an interpreter.

According to all reports, including that of Sergeant Robinson who may been in the tent or standing just outside, Cochise denied any personal knowledge of the Ward boy's capture, and added that he thought the Coyoteros (the Pinal Apaches) had taken him. If Bascom would give him 10 days, he would try to recover young Felix. Daklugie is quoted by Eve Ball in *Indeh* as saying that Ward called Cochise a liar and demanded pay for both the boy and his cattle.

From this point on, details of what happened differ, depending on whose account is believed. Bascom later wrote in his report he agreed to release Cochise, but would keep his family in custody until he returned. The Apache version, as well as those of Sergeant Robinson and other military personnel present, all agree Bascom then told Cochise everyone would be held as prisoners until the boy was recovered.

As soon as he heard this, Cochise slipped a knife out of his boot, cut a slit in the tent, and broke through the cordon of surprised soldiers who had surrounded them. Running and dodging, he made his way to safety in the nearby hills. Coyuntura also cut his way out of the tent but stumbled and was recaptured.

"To us, this story is known as 'saved by his knife,' or in Apache as *besh-yee-tsauyan*," said Kay-dah-zinne. "Cochise figured it out immediately, and that is why he knew he had to get out. He himself later said he cut his way through the tent and escaped. Many of our war leaders like Cochise would welcome someone who is honest—until the truth came out, like it did with Bascom. He tricked Cochise and lied to him. He accused Cochise of things he knew nothing about.

"I think Cochise had the same gift as Geronimo. He could see the future and knew something that was not good was going to happen. A lot of our people had that special gift. They could feel these special signs a lot of ordinary people can't feel. I know Cochise sensed harm and danger in that tent."

The next morning, Tuesday, February 5, Cochise and several of his warriors approached Bascom's camp under a white flag of truce and met the lieutenant, Ward, Sergeant Robinson, and another soldier about 150 yards from the station, not far from the edge of a large ravine. As Cochise tried to convince Bascom again that he did not have the Ward boy, three Butterfield station employees who knew Cochise, including both Culver and Wallace, apparently thought they might help convince Bascom to release his family. They slipped out of the station and started down the ravine, but unknown to them, the ravine was filled with Cochise's warriors. The three were immediately captured.

Cochise saw this and ran for cover as the Apaches in the ravine began firing at Bascom. In the melee, one Butterfield agent was killed; Culver was wounded but managed to escape. Wallace remained a prisoner. This was what Cochise wanted, and the next day he took Wallace out in front of the stage station and offered to exchange him for his family. Once more, Bascom turned him down.

Later that day, the Apaches captured a small wagon train coming into Apache Pass from the western entrance, several miles from Bascom's camp and the stage station. The wagon train included nine Mexicans and three Americans; the unfortunate Mexicans, who had no idea of the drama they had just stumbled into, were tied to their wagons that were then set on fire.

As Sweeney describes the scene, the chief then forced Wallace to write a message to Bascom, in which he offered all four of his American captives in exchange for his family: "Treat my people well and I will do the same by yours, of whom I have four." The note was "fastened to the brush," according to Sweeney, but was not retrieved for at least two days. In his report, Bascom gives the impression he received the note that very evening, but in truth it was not until several days later, and the officer never knew Cochise had captured the three other Americans.

Thus, when Cochise did not receive a reply from the lieutenant after twenty-four hours, he apparently interpreted Bascom's failure to respond as a refusal of his offer. The four prisoners were killed and their remains left along the stage road where Bascom's men would find them, although this did not happen until February 18, more than ten days later. The reason they weren't found was because Bascom thought he was still surrounded by Apaches and never sent out any patrols.

On Thursday evening, February 7, realizing he needed reinforcements as well as medical help, Bascom sent riders to both Forts Buchanan and Breckinridge, who made it through safely because Cochise and his warriors had withdrawn southward into the Chiricahuas. There he met Mangas Coloradas to plan a direct attack on the stage station in one last effort to free his family. Convincing Mangas Coloradas to join him was not difficult, since Bascom was holding Dos-the-seh, not just the wife of Cochise but Mangas's own daughter.

They attacked the station Friday morning, but pulled back after three Apaches were killed by heavy gunfire from the soldiers. With that, the warriors split up and left Apache Pass (some believe this is actually when he killed his four American captives). Cochise and his band rode to Mexico while Mangas Coloradas headed to the Gila River. Bascom's reinforcements arrived at Apache Pass on Sunday. While en route, the group from Buchanan led by Bernard Irwin captured three Apaches, thought to be Coyoteros, not Chiricahuas, and took them to the station in Apache Pass.

The Breckenridge reinforcements, led by Lieutenant Isiah N. Moore, rode in on February 14. It was only after Moore's arrival that Bascom sent out his first scouting patrol on the sixteenth, and of course they found no Apaches. What the patrol did find on the eighteenth were the mutilated bodies of the four Americans Cochise had tried to ransom for his family. The discovery sealed the fate of the Apaches, including Cochise's brother, two of his nephews, and the three Coyoteros, who were hanged the next day as Bascom, Moore, and their men rode out of Apache Pass back to Buchanan and Breckenridge. Cochise's wife and infant son were released unharmed.

Bascom's official report does not match up well with other eyewitness accounts of this historic two-week period. He completely omitted Cochise's escape from the tent, and he implied that he received the note Wallace left on the bushes near the station late on Wednesday, February 6, when in fact, the earliest he got it was on the eighth, and possibly not until even later. In his report he also left out the fact that during the brief attack on February 8, the Apaches drove off his command's forty-two mules. Most historians are in agreement Bascom did not include these items because they clearly showed his poor judgment. Nonetheless, he was commended by Lieutenant Colonel Morrison for his actions.

Bascom's blunders at Apache Pass, however, unleashed a full decade of Apache retribution against Americans. Throughout this period, Cochise repeatedly insisted that his war of retaliation had been started by his seizure in Bascom's tent and the subsequent execution of his brother and nephews. More than a few American military officers of the time agreed with Cochise, as do historians today.

Their first retaliatory strike against the Americans took place just two months later when Cochise led a war party to Stein's Peak and Doubtful Canyon along the present New Mexico-Arizona border, where they ambushed two stagecoaches and killed nine men. Within a matter of days, Cochise led additional attacks against a supply train heading out of Fort Buchanan, a detachment of troops from the fort itself, and several ranches in the Santa Cruz Valley. They not only killed any Americans they encountered but also made off with herds of cattle and horses. On one of these raids, Bascom himself was sent out to follow the Apache leader. Cochise recognized him and yelled insults at him but could never get close enough to inflict any harm.

By this time the Civil War had started, the Butterfield stage had stopped running, and as troops were transferred to faraway posts in the East, many of the forts in Apacheria were completely abandoned. The two primary American forts in southern Arizona, Buchanan and Breckenridge, were both evacuated and burned in July. The Apaches believed they truly were driving the Anglos out of their homeland, and as Cochise terrorized southern Arizona, Mangas Coloradas did the same in New Mexico, particularly around Pinos Altos, his homeland.

Later that summer the two leaders joined forces in southern New Mexico near Cooke's Peak, located about midway between the present-day cities of Deming and Hatch. At the base of the peak, Cooke's Canyon formed a narrow four-mile gap through the mountains. With a permanent water supply nearby (Cooke's Springs), the route was regularly traveled by anyone heading to or from Tucson and the Rio Grande.

It became one of the most dangerous places in either New Mexico or Arizona, with estimates of Apache victims numbering more than a hundred between 1861 and 1863. While Americans were the primary targets, virtually anyone except another Apache became a target. Seven men here. Nine more there. A supply train of wagons. Miners headed to or coming from Pinos Altos. Ranchers driving cattle through the canyon. Even military patrols.

Cooke's Canyon was not the only place Cochise made dangerous for travelers. The mines at Pinos Altos were another frequent target, as were Sylvester Mowry's Patagonia Mines not far from Tucson. No one knows how many men Mowry lost to Apache attacks and ambushes, but the number is high. Mowry himself is quoted in a letter to Colonel Joseph Rodman West in June, 1862, writing, "If the Devil would have helped me fight Apaches, I would have asked his help at any price except my soul." At Dragoon Springs, Cochise and Victorio killed four Confederate soldiers camped there in May 1862; the rock cairns marking their graves are plainly visible today.

Later in July, Cochise, Mangas Coloradas, Victorio, and their combined bands attacked an advance party of General Carleton's California Volunteers at Apache Pass. The soldiers were led by Captain Tom Roberts, who, once the Apaches triggered their ambush, unleashed a barrage of howitzer shells on them. It was later in this fighting that Mangas Coloradas was reportedly badly wounded, although Cochise continued the fight the following day until again being driven off by howitzer fire.

Roberts recommended a fort be constructed in the pass not far from the springs, and Carleton, who came through Apache Pass with the remainder of his troops about ten days later, readily agreed. Construction began on July 28, and by August 14, the first Fort Bowie had been completed and a hundred soldiers stationed there, in the heart of Cochise's homeland.

Once through Apache Pass, Carleton continued on to Santa Fe, where he took command of the Department of New Mexico, and although this would leave him somewhat removed from the battlefields of southern New Mexico and Arizona, his presence would continue to haunt the Apaches for years to come. By the autumn of 1862, as Apache raids continued, he ordered all those under his command to kill any male Apaches old enough to carry a rifle. Thus, Brigadier General Joseph Rodman West, Carleton's subordinate who had made his head-quarters in Mesilla near present-day Las Cruces, was follow-ing Carleton's instructions explicitly in January 1863 when he ordered Mangas Coloradas shot after the old chieftain had come into Fort McLane to seek peace.

If the seeds of war with the Americans had been sown by Bascom at Apache Pass barely a year earlier, then West's murder of Mangas Coloradas caused them to explode. By the summer of 1863, Cochise and his Apaches were at war with both the Americans and the Mexicans, as the state of Chihuahua, tired of the relentless raids on its villages and ranches, reinstated its bounty for Apache scalps.

In June, a lieutenant and two men were killed by Apaches while crossing the Rio Grande. The officer's body was recov-ered but not before the attackers had cut off his head, slashed open his chest, and ripped out his heart, their first real revenge for the death of Mangas Coloradas. Cochise then joined forces with Victorio and once again set up camp in Cooke's Canyon. In mid-July, they attacked a small wagon train being escorted by American soldiers, capturing three wagons and nearly two dozen mules. Two weeks later a military detachment of the California Volunteers from Las Cruces was attacked in the can-yon, resulting in the loss of wagons, mules, and supplies.

As he had done in Apache Pass, Carleton ordered the estab-lishment of a new military fort near Cooke's Canyon to try to curb the attacks, and at eleven o'clock on the night of October 2, 1863, Captain Valentine Dresher and Company B, First Infantry of the California Volunteers, arrived at Cooke's Spring to begin construction on what would become Fort Cummings. When completed, the garrison included separate quarters for officers and troops, storehouses, a hospital, a guardhouse, and corrals for more than five dozen horses, all enclosed by a ten-foot-high adobe wall.

From Cooke's Canyon, Cochise moved back to Apache Pass. Soon after, he and his warriors managed to steal all the horses from Fort Bowie. By now, Mexican forces in Sonora had taken the offensive, regularly crossing the border into Arizona and New Mexico and thus forcing the Chiricahuas to constantly stay on the move. At the same time, American forces continued their own pursuits of Cochise into Mexico. This is when Cochise's wars became more defensive than offensive, as every month he lost men, women, and children to these advancing forces.

Raiding in Mexico continued, however, largely because the Apaches could still trade horses and cattle stolen in Sonora for rifles and ammunition in the village of Janos in Chihuahua—an arrangement Cochise and other leaders had carefully nurtured for more than twenty years—but even this ended when Mexico stationed troops there permanently in 1867. Now openly pursued by both Mexican and American forces, life became a series of hit-and-run skirmishes for the Apache leader.

Realizing at last that he had no real option for the future, the Apache chieftain made several peace overtures to the Americans over the next several months, but all were refused. All Cochise and the other band leaders wanted was a reservation in their own land along with food and clothing, since their raiding would have to cease.

Thus, when Tom Jeffords led General Oliver Howard into the Cochise Stronghold in the Dragoon Mountains in the fall of 1872, the Apaches were willing to talk to him. Jeffords, who is thought to have met Cochise about two years earlier, was the only white man Cochise ever fully trusted, and certainly Howard would never have succeeded in his peace mission without Jeffords's presence. As related earlier and described by Lieutenant Sladen in his book, the men spent the next twelve days discussing and agreeing on terms of a peace between the Americans and the Apaches. The majority of the discussions took place while the men were seated on large boulders along the western side of the Stronghold; today the site is known as Council Rocks, and it is easy to imagine Cochise and Howard sitting on them.

Initially, Howard offered Cochise Alamosa Canyon in New Mexico, where he would also move Victorio's Chihenne band, but Cochise was not agreeable to that proposal. There were too many inter-tribal rivalries between them, even though both groups knew each other well and had fought together. Alamosa Canyon was Victorio's birthplace, and Cochise knew Victorio and the Chihenne were not going to leave their ancestral home and agree to move 150 miles away to Cochise's homeland.

Cochise then asked Howard to give him Apache Pass. If Howard did that, Cochise promised to halt all attacks on American forces and to also protect the roads leading into and through the pass and the immediate area.

In retrospect, the terms Cochise and Howard agreed to seem simple enough, and one wonders why none of the soldiers, agents, or bureaucrats who had ever fought or dealt with the Apaches over the years could not have agreed to the same terms. It may have been the most basic treaty ever agreed to between Indians and the American forces. The exact terms were never written or recorded at the time, although Howard did provide more details in later correspondence with the Commissioner of Indian Affairs.

Cochise received the reservation he wanted, although Howard did note it was not the reservation he himself preferred at Alamosa Canyon but that it was the only location Cochise would accept. The basic boundaries were set and recorded during his final meeting with Cochise on October 12. The Chiricahua Reservation, as it was named, extended from Dragoon Springs west of Apache Pass to Steins Peak and the New Mexico boundary, then south to the Mexican border with Sonora, and followed the border westward for fifty-five miles before turning north back to the Dragoon Mountains. Tom Jeffords was named as their Indian Agent, with primary duties to oversee the well-being of the Apaches and act as their liaison with the Americans. He had sole jurisdiction over the

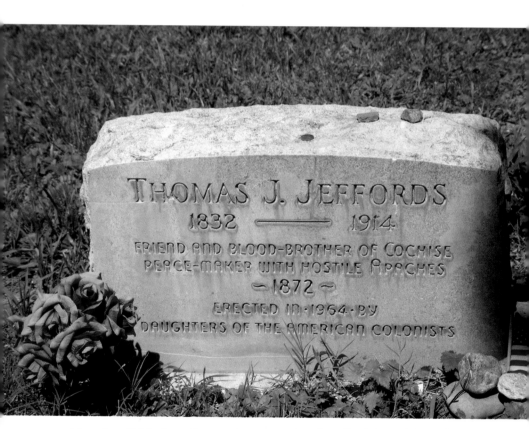

After the Chiricahua Reservation was closed, Jeffords spent several years prospecting in the area, including on his ranch north of Tucson. He died on February 19, 1914.

reservation, which meant no whites, military or civilian, could enter the reservation without his permission.

Initially, Howard was severely criticized by both the military and the press for establishing the reservation more on Cochise's terms than on his own, and particularly for the fact the military was not to set foot on the reservation. Captain Samuel Sumner, the commander at nearby Fort Bowie and who attended the treaty celebration with Howard and Cochise on October 12, was more concerned with the long border with Sonora, which would allow the Apaches to easily continue their raiding into Mexico.

Cochise countered by saying he had made peace with the Americans, not with the Mexicans, and although all hostilities against American troops and wagon trains through Apache Pass and southern Arizona ended completely, the raids into Mexico did continue, as Sumner had predicted.

Some of this was because by December, just two months after the treaty and reservation were finalized, the food and supplies promised to the Apaches failed to be delivered. Officials in Washington, specifically the Bureau of Indian Affairs and the Secretary of the Interior, simply ignored their side of the agreement as they had done in the past. It was not until General Howard himself sent a blistering letter to Washington that the promised supplies were authorized and delivered.

At the same time, the fighting between the Apaches and the Mexicans that had continued for more than two centuries could not be expected to end overnight or with the delivery of promised rations. The hatred the Apaches held for Sonora cannot begin to be understood in today's world, and had intensified for several reasons. One was the need for food and supplies, another was the repeated treachery and brutality exhibited at places like Galeana, and a third was the long memories of the Apaches and their cultural requirement for retribution.

During the initial weeks and months following the treaty, these raids into Sonora were primarily conducted by the Nednhi band of Apaches whom Cochise had asked to join him on the reservation. Their leaders were Juh and a younger firebrand warrior whose wife and family had been slain years earlier by the Mexicans. His name was Geronimo.

Cochise did not seriously try to stop them until November 1873, when it became clear the Nednhi activities were threatening the overall peace treaty he had agreed to thirteen months earlier. Unless the raiding into Sonora stopped, the military would be put in charge of the reservation. This was what the commander of the Department of Arizona, General George Crook, had wanted from the beginning. Even the War Department in Washington was calling for the reservation to be turned over to Crook, who had been forced to let General Howard proceed with his own treaty negotiations because Howard barely outranked him. He had been one of Howard's harshest critics ever since. When Juh left Cochise and returned to his own stronghold in the remote Sierra Madre of Mexico, reservation raids into Sonora ended.

Throughout his nearly two years on the Chiricahua Reservation, the treaty Cochise made with General Howard was never violated and peace reigned throughout southern Arizona. But even before Cochise met with Howard, his health had been gradually failing, and it is easy to believe he wanted the reservation to prevent the Chiricahua from being completely exterminated by the American military.

His illness was likely a type of stomach cancer, and it intensified during his months on the reservation. In his final weeks, observers noticed that he ate little and appeared to slip in and out of consciousness. Jeffords stayed by his side and provided whatever medical aid he could, but like Cochise, he sensed the end was near.

A final conversation between the two men on the evening of June 7, 1874, has been quoted often with only slight variation. Although it has been passed down by different authors for decades, it can only be attributed to Jeffords. Cochise asked

The Western side of the Cochise Stronghold rises abruptly in a wall of rocks and spires, making it easy to defend when necessary. The Dragoon Mountains extend north to south about thirty miles, but are only seven miles wide at the Stronghold.

him, "Chickasaw [Cochise's name for Jeffords], do you think you will ever see me alive again?"

"No, I do not think I will," Jeffords replied. "I think that by tomorrow night you will be dead."

"Yes, I think so too, about 10 o'clock tomorrow morning. Do you think we will ever meet again?"

A little surprised at the question, Jeffords took his time answering. "I don't know. What do you think about it?"

"I have been thinking a good deal about it while I have been sick here, and I believe we will; good friends will meet again, up there," answered Cochise.

"Where?" asked Jeffords.

"That I do not know, somewhere up there, I think," he said, pointing to the sky.

The next morning, Cochise died, as he had predicted. He was buried somewhere in the Stronghold in the Dragoon Mountains, and Jeffords may or may not have been present. If so, he never revealed the location of the grave, even though he outlived his friend by nearly forty years. To this day, no one has ever found it.

"Cochise's death created a tremendous void in Apache leadership," writes Sweeney in his acclaimed biography of the Apache chieftain. "No other leader had succeeded in obtaining a reservation in his country, one which was run by the Indians in conjunction with their agent without military interference. Perhaps no other Apache chief exhibited more wisdom, courage, fighting ability, and control of his followers than had Cochise."

Taza, the oldest son of Cochise, succeeded his father as leader of the Chiricahuas and continued to honor the treaty with General Howard. Still, he did not have the firm control over his followers his father had had, and when two drunk Apaches killed Orisoba Spence and Nicholas Rogers on April 7, 1876 at Fort Bowie for refusing to sell them any additional liquor, the fate of the Chiricahua Reservation was sealed. Washington closed the reservation and sent Taza, his brother Naiche, and most of their followers to San Carlos.

Not everyone went to San Carlos, however, and those who did not, including band leader Geronimo, continued to wage war against the Americans for another ten years, until his surrender in September 1886.

CHAPTER 8

THE AMERICANS: LIEUTENANT GEORGE N. BASCOM

To the soldiers stationed at Fort Buchanan in the years immediately preceding the Civil War, the place must have seemed like the end of the earth. Although located in Arizona's Sonoita Valley where water, grass for livestock, and sunshine were abundant, the fort was thirty miles north of the Mexican border but still at least fifty miles south of Tucson, itself hardly more than a collection of mud shacks.

Built in 1856, the buildings at Buchanan were constructed of oak planks stuck vertically into the ground, Mexican-style, and chinked with mud. They leaked during the summer rainy season and let in rattlesnakes, scorpions, and other kinds of desert life the rest of the year.

There was no protective wall of wood, rocks or even adobe bricks around the buildings, but there were standing pools of water that attracted mosquitoes and spread malaria among the troops. The food was awful and frequently in short supply. There were no nearby towns from which to purchase supplies, so scurvy was another ever-present illness. Indeed, one of the closest places to the fort that did provide occasional cattle and chickens was a ramshackle ranch twelve miles away owned by John Ward, who lived with his common-law Mexican wife and twelve-year-old son Felix. Overall, life for the soldiers at

Buchanan was boring unless they went out on the occasional patrol to look for Apaches, which they rarely found.

In the latter months of 1859, a series of raids by the Pinal, or Coyotero Apaches, who lived north of Tucson, forced Buchanan's acting commander, Captain Richard S. Ewell, to mount an expeditionary force of dragoons (the predecessors of the cavalry) into the Pinal Mountains to subdue the raiders. Ewell was wounded during the ensuing skirmishes, and in the spring of 1860 he was transferred to Fort Bliss in El Paso. His injury healed, and three years later he had become one of Robert E. Lee's primary commanders.

Ewell's replacement, Lieutenant Colonel Pitcairn Morrison, arrived at Buchanan that summer. Morrison had been stationed at Camp Floyd in northern Utah and was ready to retire after forty years in the army, but he and both the Fifth and Seventh Infantry Regiments were sent south to quell a Navajo uprising in northern Arizona. Morrison, however, and two companies of the Seventh missed the action against the Navajos when they were assigned to Fort Buchanan. With Morrison came the most inexperienced junior officer in the command, Second Lieutenant George N. Bascom.

George Nicholas Bascom was born in Owingsville, Kentucky in April or May 1837, the oldest of seven children of Sylvanus and Mary Nicholas Bascom. Mary Bascom was the daughter of Thomas Dye Owings, who, after becoming wealthy in the iron business, founded Owingsville in 1811. The town is located in Bath County in the center of the state, and today has a population of approximately 1,500. John Bell Hood, the Confederate general of Civil War fame, was born in Owingsville, where his father was a doctor, so the two families certainly knew each other.

Sylvanus Bascom died in January 1844, and his wife, unable to accept her husband's death or raise seven small children alone, was admitted into an institution, where she remained the rest of her life. George Bascom thus lost his father, mother, and siblings before he was ten years old, as the children were separated and sent to live with different families. He and one brother, Alpheus, were raised by Peter and Margaret Guerrant in Bath County.

The Bascoms had been a prominent family in the county, and so when George applied to West Point in 1853 at age seventeen, he was readily admitted. According to the Bascom Reunion Association report of March 6, 2018, he may have been inspired to attend West Point by Hood, who graduated from the Academy in 1853, a classmate of Phil Sheridan. Bascom graduated in June 1858, ranking twenty-sixth in his class of twenty-seven. That ranking put him in the infantry.

At that time, the army was organized into three broad branches, the Scientific Corps (engineers), the General Staff (quartermaster, administrative), and the Line (infantry, cavalry, artillery). Assignments into one of these three branches was based on the cadet's class ranking at the time of graduation. West Point administrators considered producing engineers for the Scientific Corps as their primary role and so the heaviest academic emphasis was placed on mathematics, the natural sciences, and both civil and military engineering.

In addition, liberal arts courses like ethics, geography, grammar, French, and Spanish were also included. Military tactics classes emphasized the old European style of massed troop formations; guerrilla fighting strategies against Indian tribes like the Apaches were not part of the curriculum.

There were numerous critics of West Point's curriculum, and many centered around whether cadets who spent four years studying mathematics and formulas could be capable soldiers in the field. Terry Mort, author of *The Wrath of Cochise* (2013), writes in his superb study of the Bascom Affair: ". . . the Academy taught conformity of thought and behavior and enforced this conformity with a rigid hierarchy, not only of officers, which is expected in any army, but of customs and values."

Lt. George Bascom had not been in Arizona very long when he first met Cochise. The incidents that followed, known as the Bascom Affair, enraged the Apache chieftain and certainly contributed to years of renewed fighting.

This, of course, leads to the basic question involving Bascom's behavior at Apache Pass: Was he properly trained and prepared to deal with the situation he encountered with Cochise? Historians have argued the answer to that question for more than 150 years.

West Point cadets were not commissioned upon graduation as they are today. Instead, when he graduated on July 1, 1858, Bascom became a brevet second lieutenant. This was an honorary rank he kept until he received his official commission in April 1859. By then he had already completed his first assignment at Fort Columbus on Governors Island, New York. Fort Columbus was a recruiting and training station for the infantry, and Bascom spent eight months there teaching new recruits the basics of military life, including how to march, load and fire their muskets, and pitch tents.

When he received his commission, he also received orders to join the Seventh Infantry Regiment at Camp Floyd in Utah, forty miles south of Salt Lake City. Two years earlier, President James Buchanan had ordered 2,500 army troops to move into Utah and to replace Mormon leader Brigham Young with a federally appointed governor. The Book of Mormon had been published in 1830, seven years before George Bascom was born, and ill feelings toward the new religion and its followers had been simmering ever since. Major issues were that the book's author, Joseph Smith, claimed he was the prophet chosen to establish God's true church. Another belief, unacceptable to many, was that polygamy, or plural marriages for men, was acceptable.

This was a time when a number of new religions started, but the Mormon doctrine created intense hatred of the religion throughout the rest of Protestant America. Violence erupted in several states, and Smith himself was attacked and murdered in Illinois. In 1847, Smith's successor, Brigham Young, led the Mormons to Utah, but in 1850 when the United States declared Utah a territory, it meant Congress could create its own government there.

They appointed Young as governor, along with six non-Mormon officials, but Young ruled as he wished. As Mort describes the situation in *The Wrath of Cochise*, "This was the beginning of constant squabbling between US officials and the Mormon hierarchy. Utah was in all respects a theocracy, regardless of what the bureaucrats from Washington said. The elders of the church, with Young at their head, ruled absolutely."

When Young declared Utah's independence, President Buchanan ordered the army west to end the rebellion. Buchanan and Young settled their differences soon after the army arrived; the Mormons accepted Albert Cumming as their new governor even though Young actually remained in power. Young also allowed the army to remain. They established Camp Floyd southwest of Salt Lake City, but tensions between all groups remained high.

The Paiute Indians of southern Utah, once aligned with the Mormons, started raiding, while in the northern part of the territory, where white settlers were pushing the Shoshoni out of their home grounds, that tribe began attacking the emigrant wagon trains. In addition, there were horse and cattle thieves among the Mormons themselves.

This is the cauldron into which Second Lieutenant Bascom arrived in the spring of 1859. But once again, quite possibly because he was the least experienced junior officer in the Seventh Regiment, he did not see any Indian action. He did see his first Indians—Goshutes, or Diggers as most called them, who spent their days lolling lazily around Camp Floyd or in the desert hunting food, which consisted of snakes, insects, and roots. Bascom himself left no written accounts of life at Camp Floyd, but as the most junior officer he would probably have been tasked with very basic troop training duties similar to those he had performed at Fort Columbus.

One diversion at Camp Floyd may have been the opportunity to lead patrols outside the walls to protect army survey teams (those West Point engineers) improving the roads for the waves of emigrants coming west. Bascom likely encountered Goshutes on these patrols, as well, and Mort hypothesizes that seeing these particular Indians may have produced feelings of loathing and contempt in him, strengthening his beliefs in the superiority of the white race. "It's reasonable to suppose that Bascom, having seen the Goshutes, would have extrapolated an attitude toward Indians that would have reinforced his natural prejudices reflecting the widespread white view that all Indians were not only obviously inferior," he writes, "but also essentially the same."

In the summer of 1860, after Bascom had been at Camp Floyd just over a year, the Fifth and Seventh Regiments were ordered to New Mexico Territory. Bascom and two companies of the Seventh Infantry, under the leadership of Lieutenant Colonel Morrison, were sent to Fort Buchanan, where they arrived in October. The Fifth Infantry, along with the remainder of the Seventh, went out to fight the Navajos, who had attacked another installation, Fort Defiance in northern Arizona (at this time, the New Mexico Territory included most of present-day Arizona).

Another fort, Fort Breckinridge, had been established north of Tucson in May 1860. It was in rough, mountainous country south of where the Coyotero Apaches lived. That band naturally became frustrated with the growing numbers of white settlers moving into their ancestral hunting lands and started raiding the emigrant trains and newly built farms and ranches. This is when Captain Ewell was sent out to set things straight with the Coyoteros and was wounded.

On January 27, 1861, the Coyoteros simply bypassed Breckinridge and came into the Sonoita Valley, where they attacked John Ward's little hardscrabble ranch. Ward himself was not present at the time, but young Felix was, and the Apaches took him captive. When Ward returned to the ranch and realized what had happened, he immediately rode to Fort Buchanan, where Morrison ordered Second Lieutenant George Bascom to head out and find the trail of the raiders.

Upon reaching the Ward ranch, Bascom determined that the Apache trail led eastward (the Coyoteros had also stolen Ward's twenty cattle, so the trail was easy to find) toward Apache Pass, well known as the home of Cochise. Bascom returned to the fort and reported his findings to Morrison. It did not seem to register with either officer that Apache Pass was seventy miles away and that the Coyoteros might start in that direction and then turn northward again to bypass Fort Breckinridge.

Indeed, a few days later, Bascom, now commanding a patrol of fifty-four infantrymen, all on mules, did miss the Coyotero trail heading north. He and the patrol continued to Apache Pass and set up camp in Siphon Canyon, several hundred yards from the stage station. Cochise arrived the next afternoon, February 4, which was when the Bascom Affair started.

By February 19 it was over, at least for the time being. Bascom and his men headed west toward Fort Buchanan, reaching the fort on February 23. In his official report, written on February 25, he omitted several major issues, including Cochise's escape from the tent. Still, Morrison accepted it as Bascom wrote it.

Just two months later, the Civil War began. Under orders from Washington, both Buchanan and Breckinridge were abandoned and the troops moved to Fort Craig to defend against an expected Confederate invasion into the Rio Grande Valley. Bascom and the Seventh Infantry were among those ordered to Craig, and on February 20–21 he and some 3,000 Union troops met 2,500 Confederates at Valverde, a crossing on the Rio Grande a few miles north of Fort Craig. By this time, Bascom had been promoted to captain and was in command of Company C of the Seventh Infantry.

His company and Company F suffered some of the Seventh's heaviest casualties as the Confederates pushed forward and forced the Union soldiers back across the river to the fort. During a truce called by Craig's commanding officer, Colonel Edward Canby, to recover the dead and wounded, Bascom's body was found on a sandbar in the river. He was one of five Union officers killed that day.

"There is no doubt Bascom made serious mistakes in Apache Pass, and that all of them were, if not predictable, certainly unsurprising," concludes Mort. "Bascom was a representative of his culture, the white civilization, and the culture of the army . . . when he encountered the strange and imposing Cochise, Bascom most likely became uneasy and fell back on what he knew—giving orders and demanding that they be obeyed . . . He wanted to make a name for himself, no doubt, but even more important, he wanted to avoid failure."

George Bascom was killed during the battle at Valverde in February 1862 and buried at Fort Craig. When Fort Craig was closed in 1885, the bodies were reinterred at the Santa Fe National Cemetery. His body could not be identified, however, and is one of many with an "Unknown" headstone there.

Bascom was buried in the cemetery at Fort Craig, and when the fort was closed in 1885, the bodies were reburied in the Santa Fe National Cemetery. His body could not be identified and is one of many with an "Unknown" headstone there.

To the end of his own life, Cochise blamed Bascom for the years of bloody conflict that followed. Did he ever learn of Bascom's death at Valverde? There is no official record that anyone ever told him, but certainly, if he had not heard, then General Howard probably told him during their peace talks on the flat rocks in the Stronghold almost a dozen years later.

CHAPTER 9

PLACES TO SEE: FORT BOWIE NATIONAL HISTORIC SITE

For more than two decades, Fort Bowie served as the primary center of military operations against the Chiricahua Apaches. Located on a strategic travel route through the Chiricahua Mountains known as Apache Pass, the Spanish called it Puerto del Dado, the Pass of Chance, because of the danger of moving through the home of Cochise.

There were actually two installations. The first, built during the summer of 1862, consisted of just thirteen tents surrounded by rough stone fortifications. It was named after Colonel George Washington Bowie, and took less than three weeks to establish.

The second fort, the ruins of which are still standing about three hundred yards southeast of the original, was started in 1868 and eventually grew to number nearly forty rock, wood, and adobe structures. For more than twenty years, soldiers stationed here fought not only Cochise but also Geronimo. Fort Bowie remained open as an active army post for eight additional years after Geronimo's surrender in 1886, until it was abandoned in 1894. Known today as the Fort Bowie Historic Site, visitors here will find the remnants of the fort's walls; a small, modern National Park Service visitor center and museum; and drinking water.

The trail also passes beside Apache Springs, the permanent water supply that made Apache Pass so important. Although a water control structure has been placed over the spring to redirect the water, the spring still flows freely today. The Battle of Apache Pass between the Apaches and Brigadier General James Carleton took place here July 15–16, 1862.

A small, lonely, wrought iron–enclosed cemetery a hundred yards from the stage station ruins contains the graves of a number of civilians who lived or worked at the fort, several of them killed by the Apaches. All military personnel and their dependents who had been buried there were moved to the National Cemetery in San Francisco in March 1895.

Fort Bowie was another of the military posts established to control the Apaches, primarily Cochise. Located in Apache Pass, these are the ruins of the second Fort Bowie, built in 1868. The first fort, built in 1862, consisted largely of tents enclosed by a stone wall.

Among the graves remaining in the cemetery in Apache Pass is that of Orisoba Spence, one of the two white men killed by the Apaches when they refused to sell them liquor on the Chiricahua Reservation created by Cochise and General Howard; their deaths led to the closing of the reservation. Spence was awarded the Medal of Honor for his earlier fighting against the Apaches while serving in the Eighth US Cavalry.

IN MEMORY
of
LITTLEROBE
Son of
GERONIMO
Apache Chief
Died Sept. 10, 1885
Age 2 Years

Another grave in the cemetery in Apache Pass is that of Little Robe, a son of Geronimo who had been brought to Fort Bowie after being captured by Mexicans.

Among the twenty-one remaining graves is that of Orisoba Spence, a private with Company G of the Eighth Cavalry, who was awarded the Medal of Honor for gallantry in an engagement against Cochise's Apaches on October 20, 1869. After leaving the army, he worked as a civilian at Fort Bowie, and was killed by Indians on April 7, 1876, along with Nicholas M. Rogers, whose grave is beside that of Spence's. Rogers had been known to sell whiskey to the Apaches, and on that day, several of them came to buy more. Spence was there, and when the two men refused to sell the Indians any additional liquor, both were killed.

Three small Apache children, including the two-year-old son of Geronimo, Little Robe, are also buried here. The three died while being held at the fort in 1885. Little Robe was among a group of fifteen Apache women and children captured in Mexico and brought to Fort Bowie, where he is believed to have died of dysentery.

To reach the trailhead on Apache Pass Road, take Exit 362 off I-10 at the town of Bowie, and follow the signs to Fort Bowie. The route will take you south for twelve miles on a paved road (part is unpaved) to a large, well-marked gravel parking lot, actually in Apache Pass. An alternate route is to follow AZ Highway 186 south from the city of Wilcox (also on I-10) for twenty-two miles, then turning east on the gravel road leading into Apache Pass and to the trailhead parking lot. This is the same road described above.

For current park hours, visit www.nps.gov/fobo/index.htm, or telephone the park visitor center at (520) 847–2500.

CHAPTER 10

THE APACHES: VICTORIO AND NANA

A s the Apaches watched the long line of blue-coated soldiers and their supply wagons move slowly down the narrow, cottonwood-lined trail leading toward Pinos Altos, it is doubtful any of them truly understood the significance of what they were seeing. Not Mangas Coloradas, the powerful and highly revered chief of the Mimbrenos band, into whose homeland the soldiers were marching; not Cuchillo Negro, the principal chief of the Warm Springs band; and certainly not Cuchillo Negro's close associate and chosen successor, a tall, well-proportioned young warrior named Bi-duye, whom history would soon know by the name given to him by his Mexican enemies: Victorio.

No one recorded exactly who or how many warriors accompanied Mangas Coloradas that day; there were probably between two and three dozen. It is likely several other tribal leaders were also present, including one named Kas-tzi-den. His name is believed to mean "Broken Foot," and was bestowed on him due to an injury that never healed properly. Later, he would become known to the Americans simply as Nana.

Nana was almost certainly a member of the Chihenne band, which would put him into constant contact with both Cuchillo Negro and Victorio. The late historian Dan L. Thrapp, who studied and wrote extensively about the Chiricahua, put Nana's birth sometime before 1810, which would make him as much as twenty years younger than Mangas, whom Thrapp believed was born about 1790, but probably a decade older than Victorio. While Mangas Coloradas was recognizable for his extraordinary height of about six feet, five inches, Nana was known for the very noticeable limp from his foot injury. Some historians believe he may have married one of Victorio's sisters.

It was Sunday, October 18, 1846, and while these were not the first white soldiers the three Apaches had seen, it was by far the largest group they had ever encountered. Just six months earlier, on May 12, the United States had declared war on Mexico, and President James Polk had sent General Stephen Watts Kearny to New Mexico with orders to claim the territory and create a provisional government to prevent possible Spanish uprisings. Kearny and his army had arrived in Santa Fe on August 18, raised the American flag over the Palace of Governors on the town square, and appointed Charles Bent as the territory's first governor.

For years, America had been trying to purchase California but had repeatedly been refused. Now, Kearny was on his way to California to claim that territory for the United States, as well. He knew he would be going into the heart of Apacheria, as well as across essentially unknown country before he reached Los Angeles, so before leaving Santa Fe he had hired veteran mountain man Thomas "Broken Hand" Fitzpatrick as his guide. Fitzpatrick had led the army south following the Rio Grande, then, just below Socorro they had made their westward turn.

They'd entered Mangas Coloradas's country the moment they'd turned to the west, and that evening Mangas, Cuchillo Negro, and Victorio rode into Kearny's camp at Santa Lucia Spring, a dozen miles west of the Santa Rita del Cobre mines. They greeted the general and gifts were exchanged, especially after the Apaches learned Kearny had come to fight their mutual enemy. To their utter amazement, however, Kearny refused their assistance in fighting the Mexicans unless they stopped their raiding into Sonora and Chihuahua.

The Apaches had been raiding in Mexico for decades, so much so that it had become not just a lifestyle but also a semi-profitable necessity. The targets were most often smaller villages and isolated ranches where cattle, horses, and other stock were taken, generally to be traded in the Chihuahuan town of Janos. There, where the Indians and townspeople maintained a peaceful relationship strictly because of this trading, the Apaches received blankets, food, knives, rifles, and ammunition in exchange for their stolen goods. Even though ranchers and settlers were frequently killed during these raids, the town of Janos was spared.

What neither the young Victorio nor the older chiefs with him that fateful October day did not and could not understand was that Kearny and his army represented the actual beginning of America's new ideology of westward expansion. This was Manifest Destiny in its most basic form, a mixture of expansionist fervor, patriotism, and religious doctrine. It had already taken over the eastern half of the country, and President Polk had declared a war on Mexico to gain the western half.

The war with Mexico ended on February 2, 1848, and among the provisions included in the Treaty of Guadalupe Hidalgo was one that committed America to halting the Apache raids into Mexico. This provision, however, was not as far-reaching as was the transfer of much of the Southwest into the possession of the United States.

Travel across Apacheria started quickly, and Indian raids into Mexico grew accordingly, as the Apaches realized the very settlers crossing their land en route to the California gold fields after the discovery at Sutter's Mill needed fresh livestock. This was when Mexican authorities once again attacked a band of Apaches camped near Janos and murdered mainly women and children, including the mother, wife, and children of Geronimo.

Thus, Victorio and Nana watched as the landscape of Alamosa Canyon and indeed the entire face of Apacheria began to change. For one thing, territorial status required a military presence, and the first commander of the military in New Mexico, Lieutenant Colonel Edwin Sumner, arrived in 1851, when Victorio was about twenty-five. Sumner began establishing a series of forts and outposts across the territory, and in less than a decade sixteen such forts had been built. Two of the most important of these were Forts Thorn and Craig along the Rio Grande, both of which would soon play a major role in the lives of Victorio and Nana.

The federal government's practice of appointing Indian Agents also took effect. It was done through a department known as the Indian Office. Corruption started immediately. Virtually none of the agents appointed to deal with the Apaches had any experience whatsoever, even though they were responsible for the monumental tasks of creating treaties, moving the Indians to reservations, and then distributing food and supplies to them. The first such agent for the Apaches had actually shown up in 1849 and several had followed him, since most rarely stayed once they realized what the job entailed.

In April 1853, the new territorial governor, William Lane, who had been appointed upon the death of New Mexico's first formal governor, James S. Calhoun, a year earlier, managed to negotiate a treaty with Victorio and the Chihenne Apaches. In return for receiving regular allotments of beef, cattle, horses, and corn, the Apaches agreed to stop raiding and to move into a sparsely settled region west of the Mimbres River, about twenty miles east of present-day Silver City. This, of course, was an area they knew well and which was off the main travel routes.

The following year, former military physician Michael Steck was named as the Indian Agent for the Apaches, and the first thing he discovered was that none of the promised rations had been delivered because Governor Lane had spent all the funds set aside to pay for them. For that first year, Victorio and his band had survived by hunting elk, deer, and antelope, but Steck knew it couldn't continue. He realized he needed to

This is the only known photograph of Victorio. Some believe he was being forcibly restrained as the photograph was being taken. He was born sometime during the 1820s, and even before the American Civil War began he was pleading for a reservation for his Chihenne in Alamosa Canyon, but officials in Washington never approved it. *Arizona Historical Society*

create a permanent reservation for Victorio to eliminate further encroachment into their land and preserve the fragile peace that already showed signs of breaking.

Raids into Mexico started again, and one band of Apaches even struck ranches in the Mesilla Valley near present-day Las Cruces. In most instances these were subsistence raids for cattle, horses, and mules necessary for their survival, but at the same time the US military considered them hostile acts and took the offensive against the Apaches. "The failure to stop the depredations only served to increase the hostile feelings on both sides," writes William S. Kiser in *Dragoons in Apacheland*. "By 1856, military action began to precede any treaty negotiations."

Tensions continued to increase and military campaigns, primarily out of Forts Thorn and Craig, became both larger and more frequent. Because the majority of these long-range patrols, many of them lasting several weeks, generally failed to even see the marauding Indians, virtually any Apaches encountered were considered the enemy.

Thus, when Colonel William Loring and his frustrated troops attacked an Apache camp deep in the rugged canyons of southern New Mexico not all that far from Fort Thorn on May 24, 1857, they never realized they were shooting at one of the most peaceful Apache bands in the entire region. Cuchillo Negro was among those killed, and upon his death, Victorio assumed a greater leadership role even while continuing to serve under Mangas Coloradas.

Loring's patrol was part of what has become known as the Gila Campaign, a larger, three-month-long foray into Apacheria led by Colonel Benjamin L. Bonneville. Born near Paris, France on April 14, 1796, Bonneville had come to America to be a soldier and had graduated from West Point in 1815. He had served in the Mexican War and would also see action later in the Civil War, but he is better known for his explorations in the Rocky Mountains during the fur trade era of the 1830s.

Bonneville Pass, near Dubois, Wyoming, is named for him, as are the Bonneville Salt Flats in Utah.

His Gila Campaign, however, was considered a total failure in that the only thing it accomplished was to bring even more retaliatory strikes by the Apaches. One of Bonneville's officers, writing in his diary, described the entire expedition as a "campaign of clowns," and Kiser sums it more chillingly, noting that "the Gila Campaign would forever alter the manner in which the Apaches and the Americans viewed their conflict with one another."

When the Santa Rita copper mines reopened in 1858, and with virtually no cooperation from either the territorial governor in Santa Fe nor the Indian Office in Washington, Agent Steck moved forward on his own and established a new Apache agency and reservation further to the east on the Alamosa River. This was where Victorio had been born and always wanted a reservation, and Steck named it the Warm Springs Agency, but because the Indian Office refused to take any action to make it official, encroachment continued.

Then, that May, Jacob Snively made his gold strike in Bear Creek, right in the heart of the Apache homeland. This led to the establishment of the town of Silver Springs later that year, but hostilities began again almost immediately. Whenever any of Victorio's men left the area to hunt game, they themselves became fair game for nearby miners and ranchers. Steck became so frustrated with Washington's lack of action he resigned, and Victorio lost perhaps the only white friend he would ever have. Steck was replaced by an agent named Pinckney Tully.

By now, Victorio was between thirty-five and forty years old and in the best condition of his life, both physically and mentally. He was described as tall, "but not nearly as tall as Mangas Coloradas," writes Kathleen Chamberlain in her biography of the Apache warrior, *Victorio* (2007), "and some considered him handsome." His expression was usually calm and even serene, but others described him as aloof, calculating, and distrusting.

Some Americans who knew him said his piercing dark eyes could look straight through a person without ever changing, making it practically impossible to know what Victorio was actually thinking.

The names of his parents are not known, nor if his father may have been a chief, which would have opened the door to Victorio's inheritance of the position. Even if this had been the case, Victorio would still have had to prove himself capable of leadership. Nana, more than a decade his senior and far more experienced, readily stepped aside to let him become the leader of their band, which does give some credence to the possibility his lineage may have been one of leadership.

At 4:30 a.m. on April 12, 1861, far to the east of Alamosa Canyon on an artificial island in a place named Charleston Harbor, a crusty, long-haired old soldier from Virginia named Edmund Ruffin changed the world once again for Victorio, Mangas Coloradas, and Cochise when he fired the first cannon shot aimed at Fort Sumter and with it started the Civil War. Within days, the American military began closing forts all across Apacheria and leaving to fight other battles a thousand miles away.

The three chieftains, who believed they had finally driven the hated White Eyes out of their homeland, quickly joined their bands and began raiding the abandoned forts, ranches, and even Silver City and Pinos Altos. Only a few weeks earlier, Cochise had been enraged by the insolent behavior of young Lieutenant George Bascom, and now they could all vent their rage and revenge while still traveling freely. Geronimo joined them as well, and by June, Victorio and the others had essentially regained complete control of southern New Mexico and Arizona between the Mesilla Valley and Tucson.

One of the young ranchers the Apaches had forced out of the region was Sherod Hunter, a native of Tennessee who had resettled along the Mimbres River in March 1857 after losing both his wife and infant son soon after childbirth. In May

1861, he joined Captain George Frazer's company of Arizona Rangers, based in Mesilla, New Mexico. The company was part of Brigadier General Henry H. Sibley's 2,500-man brigade of Texas troops.

The following January, Sibley ordered Hunter, now a captain, on a dual mission that likely suited the twenty-eight-year-old officer perfectly: he and the seventy-five men under him were to occupy Tucson and protect the pro-Confederate citizens in the area from Apache attacks. At the same time, they were to watch for and engage any Union troops attempting to enter Arizona from the west.

Sibley himself, with the full approval of Jefferson Davis, planned to march the remainder of his men up the Rio Grande into Colorado and take control of the gold and silver mines there. That accomplished, he would then move his force west to California and capture the gold fields near Sacramento.

The riches thus gained would not only add immeasurably to the Confederate treasury but also open a new supply route across the Southwest, thwarting the Union blockade of both the Gulf and Atlantic coasts. Sibley would be using Hunter's Arizona Rangers as an early warning system to alert him of any Union troop movements coming eastward from California.

Troops did approach from the west, the so-called California Column led by General James H. Carleton. Hunter's men fought two brief engagements with them, at Stanwix Station and again at Picacho Pass. A few days later, on May 5, a small detachment of Hunter's men were ambushed by Victorio, Cochise, and perhaps as many as a hundred Apaches while they were camped at the abandoned Butterfield Overland Mail Station at Dragoon Springs, about fifteen miles east of the present-day town of Benson, Arizona.

The Apaches killed four of the soldiers and captured more than four dozen horses and mules. It was not a major engagement by any means, but rather a reminder of how much the Apaches hated the Americans, regardless of which color of uniform they wore. Four days later, Sherod Hunter and his men counterattacked the Apaches, killing five and recovering all their lost livestock. Then they buried the four soldiers a few yards away from the rock walls of the old stage station.

One warm, windy July afternoon, I walked beside the remains of that Dragoon Springs stage station and the rock cairns that still mark the graves of those four soldiers. It is a lonely, desolate place on a barren, rocky hill where even the slightest breeze ruffles the small Confederate flags at the foot of each cairn. The graves are in a neat row just a few feet apart, but only two are positively identified; the names of the other two soldiers lost forever to history. They are the only Confederate soldiers known to have been killed in Arizona.

On February 21, 1862, a brutally cold, overcast day, Sibley's larger force won an engagement at Valverde, a shallow, sandy Rio Grande crossing south of Socorro and only seven miles north of Fort Craig. In a strange twist of history, the fight at Valverde matched Sibley against his close friend and former West Point classmate, Colonel Edward Canby, commander of Fort Craig. Canby had been the best man at Sibley's wedding and he himself had married a cousin of Sibley's wife. In his book *Blood and Thunder* (2006), esteemed author Hampton Sides quotes a Union soldier's description of Canby as "tall and straight, coarsely dressed, his countenance hard and weather beaten, a cigar in his mouth which he never lights."

Sibley, by contrast, was known as "the Walking Whiskey Keg," according to Sides, because of his excessive drinking. Nonetheless, as a career army officer, he had served with distinction on the frontier as well as in the earlier War with Mexico. In truth, Sibley wasn't even in the battle at Valverde because he was too drunk to ride a horse.

The battle took place at the Valverde crossing because Canby fooled his friend by cutting down and trimming a number of large pine trees, painting them black, and placing them on the fort's walls to look like cannons. He did this because Sibley had nearly twice as many trained army regulars as he did; the majority of his four-thousand-man force at Craig were untrained volunteers, many of whom spoke only Spanish.

These particular men, the First New Mexico Volunteers, were commanded by the former fur trapper and guide Colonel Kit Carson, who not only spoke fluent Spanish but who, like Canby, also knew Sibley personally. The fighting was fierce and turned into desperate hand-to-hand combat until finally, as his casualties continued to mount, Canby ordered a retreat.

The next morning, both leaders declared a truce so they could retrieve their wounded and bury their dead; bodies of men and horses covered both sides of the river. Union forces

The rock cairns of four Confederate soldiers who Cochise, Victorio, and others killed at Dragoon Springs are still visible, as are the nearby ruins of the stage station. These four men were the only four Confederate soldiers known to have been killed by the Apaches in Arizona.

reported 263 dead, wounded, or missing, while Confederate losses totaled about two hundred. Tactically, the battle went down in history as a Confederate victory.

Three weeks later, Sibley's forces gained control of Santa Fe, which by then was almost deserted. A week later, again with Sibley avoiding the battlefield, the Confederates were defeated in two days of hard fighting on the Santa Fe Trail at Glorieta Pass, about thirty miles west of Santa Fe.

On the afternoon of the second day of fighting, Union forces discovered Sibley's lightly guarded supply train and completely destroyed it, along with hundreds of horses and mules. The Union officer responsible for this was Major John Milton Chivington, who two years later would become far more infamously known as the architect of the Sand Creek Massacre, in which 230 peaceful Cheyenne and Arapaho, the majority women and children, were killed.

With the loss of all his supplies and equipment, Sibley retreated south to Mesilla and then back into Texas, thus ending the Confederate invasion. In his place came a far worse nightmare for Victorio. General Carleton was an avowed Indian hater who, with the Confederate threat now over, could devote all his energy to eliminating the Apaches.

The first battle of Apache Pass took place in mid-July, when Carleton sent Captain Thomas Roberts with an advance guard of 126 men, twenty-two wagons of supplies, and two hundred hundred head of stock to secure the springs in the pass for his main column that would follow in a week. Roberts's troops were ambushed by Victorio, Cochise, and Mangas Coloradas as they approached the spring, but the captain had also brought with him something the Apaches had never seen before, heavy field artillery in the form of two howitzers, which Roberts quickly began using.

Mangas Coloradas was wounded, and Victorio and the other Apaches retreated. On July 28, Carleton led his remaining men safely through the pass. He ordered the construction of a fort in the pass to safeguard against future Apache attacks. This became Fort Bowie.

Carleton also stationed some of his troops at Pinos Altos to protect the miners there, and in January 1863, Mangas Coloradas rode into the encampment to negotiate a peace treaty with General Joseph West, whom Carleton had put in charge. As described earlier, the chief was instead immediately taken prisoner and shot and killed later that night. Upon his death, Victorio took over full leadership of the Chihenne band, with Nana beside him.

As the Civil War intensified in the East, Washington did nothing to stop Carleton from trying to eliminate the different Indian tribes in New Mexico, but as he initiated his grand scheme of consolidating each of the Indian tribes in New Mexico at Bosque Redondo, Victorio and the Chihenne continued to live relatively undisturbed at Warm Springs. When Michael Steck, by then superintendent of Indian Affairs for all of New Mexico, approached them about Bosque Redondo, Victorio naturally refused to go.

Carleton, born in 1814 in Castine, Maine, near Penobscot Bay, had originally wanted to be a novelist. He had been attracted to the American West, particularly to the various Indian tribes, after reading the works of James Fenimore Cooper, but in the spring of 1839 he joined the army. He apparently loved military life on the frontier and fought in the Mexican War with General Zachary Taylor in the battle of Buena Vista, among other engagements. Taylor went on to become president, while Carleton, who entered the war as a lieutenant, came out as a major. His career path was set.

In 1852, while leading a military expedition to explore the Pecos River in New Mexico, he had found a broad valley where the river made an abrupt bend and the banks were lined with thick, heavy cottonwoods and the water was filled with waterfowl. Unknown to Carleton at that moment, the spot had long been known to the Mescalero Apaches, the Comanches, and even the earliest Spanish explorers, who had named it Bosque Redondo, or the Round Forest, because of how the cotton-woods grew there. He could never forget it, even after he was transferred to Fort Tejon in California.

Carleton had met Kit Carson the previous year, and the two men had remained friends. In 1862, when he led the California Column through Apache Pass on his way to counteract Sibley's Confederate invasion, Carleton was likely thinking of what he could accomplish there. He'd been promoted to brigadier general, and in September 1862, with the Confederate threat eliminated, he had been named commander of the Ninth Military Department, with headquarters in Santa Fe.

Throughout this time, the Navajo had been more than restless. Just like the Apaches in the mountains and forests to their south, they had seen the steady influx of white settlers taking over their land. Fighting and raiding had escalated, and Carleton determined to put a stop to it. He ordered a fort, Fort Sumner, to be built at Bosque Redondo where he would force all the Navajo to live, where he would teach them to be farmers. It became his grand plan, the crowning glory of his career.

First, however, he'd begin with the Mescalero Apaches, and he knew just whom to send to round them up: Kit Carson. Among his instructions to Carson were orders to kill all the adult men whenever and wherever he found them. With the Mescaleros under control, he could then systematically move from tribe to tribe.

Carson didn't want the job, and when he was forced to take it, he did not follow Carleton's orders. By November 1862, the Mescalero had been forced to surrender. The Mescalero leader, Cadete, spoke to Carleton in Santa Fe, and his speech for the tribe is recorded by Sides in *Blood and Thunder.*

"Your weapons are better than ours," said the Mescalero chieftain. "We are worn out. We have no provisions, no means to live. Your troops are everywhere . . . You have driven us from our last and best stronghold, and we have no more heart. Do with us as may seem good to you, but do not forget we are men and braves."

The Navajo were next, and Carson brought them in, after Carleton refused his resignation. The former scout had come to believe that the majority of Indian troubles in the West were caused by aggressions by whites, but somehow Carleton made him go.

In the end, by 1865, more than nine thousand Navajo had surrendered to Carson and his men and were marched across New Mexico to Bosque Redondo. The "reservation," if it could be called that, was forty miles square, but the cottonwoods that had originally captured Carleton's eye occupied only a small portion of it. Overall, the land was hot, dry, and completely uninhabited.

The place was chosen because of this remoteness; it was never designed to be a military fort for defense of wagon trains and settlers. There was seldom enough food to go around, except when Charles Goodnight delivered herds of cattle, and the Pecos was so alkaline in that area it made all who drank its waters sick.

Steck and Carleton were having constant disagreements at this time about how to manage the Indians, and one has to wonder just how strongly the agent urged Victorio to even try living at Bosque Redondo. Steck had, in fact, declared Carleton's massive spending there—nearly a million dollars the first year—as a huge waste. At last, in September 1866, after several investigations ordered by Secretary of War Edwin Stanton and a personal visit by General Sherman, Carleton was relieved and Bosque Redondo closed. The Mescalero had already escaped back to southern New Mexico about a hundred miles from the bosque; the Navajo walked on foot four hundred miles back to their beloved red rock canyons in northern New Mexico and Arizona.

By this time, Steck was completely worn out from the frustration of dealing with Washington's bureaucrats. Not long after Carleton was dismissed at Bosque Redondo, he himself retired for good from the Indian Service and left the Southwest.

"Carleton probably did more damage to Apache and white relations than the Bascom affair and the murder of Mangas Coloradas combined," writes Chamberlain. "His support for mining on Indian land, his permission to soldiers to prospect for gold while on duty, and the Bosque Redondo failure had dramatically increased unrest, distrust, and violence."

Through all of this, Victorio continued to ask Steck to make the Warm Springs Reservation a permanent home for the Chihenne, but he never received a reply. Victorio didn't exactly help his cause when, on May 4, 1866, his warriors stole thirty cavalry horses from Fort Craig and a month later drove off another three dozen head from another military base.

More Indian agents came and went, but none could provide Victorio and his people rations on a regular basis. Finally, in the spring of 1872, more than a decade after Agent Michael Steck had begged Washington for a permanent reservation in Alamosa Canyon, officials made a decision, but it was not Alamosa Canyon. Instead, they decided on the Tularosa Valley, some ninety miles northwest of Alamosa. The land there was not well suited for growing crops, but the area was more remote than Alamosa Canyon and would lessen the interactions between the Apaches and encroaching whites. That very remoteness, however, also increased the difficulties of supplying Victorio's people with rations, so in essence the same basic problems remained unresolved.

That summer, as part of Grant's faltering Peace Policy, General Oliver Howard made his trip west to visit Cochise. En route, he stopped at Tularosa and talked with Victorio, who took the one-armed general down to Alamosa Canyon. Howard agreed that Alamosa was a better choice for a reservation, but the only new reservation he created was the Great Chiricahua Reservation for Cochise after the two met at the Stronghold. Howard later defended his action by stating that any reservation in Alamosa Canyon had to include Cochise and that the chief refused to move, but this was never explained to Victorio.

At last, in April 1874, Victorio and his people were allowed to return to Alamosa Canyon, but more problems arose. Geronimo, becoming more and more active in raiding, began using the reservation as his headquarters, and even Victorio himself continued to raid into Mexico. Likewise, the Mescaleros, whose reservation had been established on May 29, 1873, on the eastern side of the Rio Grande, also experienced food shortages and raided local ranches and farms. On the Great Chiricahua Reservation in southern Arizona, Taza's young warriors intensified their raiding, as well.

The previous year, the Indian Office in Washington had actually made the decision to move all the Apaches once again, this time to San Carlos, where they could be more easily controlled by military forces at nearby Fort Apache. The Great Chiricahua Reservation was closed in the autumn of 1876 and while many of those Chiricahua were moved to San Carlos, others escaped to join Victorio at Warm Springs.

General George Crook had been the commanding officer at Fort Apache since 1871 and he felt the army should be in total charge of controlling the Apaches. He'd been fighting and subduing different Indian tribes across the West for more than a decade and felt the only way to stop the Apaches from raiding was through strict military action against any warriors found off the reservation.

The Indian agent assigned to San Carlos was John P. Clum, who arrived on August 8, 1874. "He was twenty-two years old when he set foot on the reservation for the first time," notes Chamberlain in *Victorio*. "A New York native, he had no experience whatsoever in dealing with Indians." Clum had come to New Mexico in hopes the dry climate would help his rheumatoid arthritis. Naturally, he and Crook clashed from the beginning.

Subsistence raiding continued. Just as Taza had had trouble controlling his own young warriors, so did Victorio, who had been trying to live peacefully at Warm Springs. In May 1877, Clum was ordered to Warm Springs to move Victorio and his band to San Carlos. One of the first things the agent had initiated at San Carlos was to form an Apache police force, and he brought more than a hundred of them with him when he approached Victorio's camp. Victorio and 343 members of his band surrendered peacefully and headed to San Carlos.

Although Clum seemed to be sympathetic to the plight of the Apaches, he continued to clash with the military over a variety of issues, primarily the continuous shortage of rations. On July 1 he resigned, and one dark night a few weeks later Victorio, Nana, and more than three hundred others slipped off the reservation as well. Nana made it across the Rio Grande to the Mescalero Reservation, while Victorio, heading north to avoid Crook's military patrols, eventually made it to Fort Wingate near the present-day city of Grants, New Mexico, where, completely out of supplies and tired of dodging the seemingly endless military patrols, he surrendered.

In early November, Brigadier General John Pope, commander of the Department of the Missouri, agreed to let the Apache chieftain and his band return to Alamosa Canyon. Even hard-line General Phil Sheridan agreed that returning Victorio to Alamosa Canyon was a good move. Colonel Edward Hatch, stationed in Santa Fe as district commander and in whose district Alamosa Canyon was located, agreed and petitioned officials in Washington to allow Victorio to settle permanently at Ojo Caliente. The petition was refused.

Victorio and his band stayed in their beloved homeland until late the following summer, when Secretary of the Interior Carl Schurz, showing his total lack of understanding of the Apache situation in the Southwest, again ordered them to San Carlos, continuing his draconian policy of Indian concentration. Instead of returning to the dry, desolate Arizona reservation, however, Victorio, with forty-four warriors and perhaps fifty women and children, headed into the mountains. For the next few months, he and his small band hid, eluding troops while alternating between Chihuahua, Sonora, Alamosa Canyon, and finally the Mescalero Reservation, where he again surrendered.

It was now June 1879, and Victorio was a wanted man. He knew it, and on August 21, he fled the Mescaleros and once again returned to the only place he'd ever wanted to live, Alamosa Canyon. Chamberlain and other historians wonder if Victorio thought that by continually returning there he might somehow convince authorities to let him remain. Indeed, even General Sherman, who had been fighting the Apaches practically since the end of the Civil War, agreed with Sheridan that Warm Springs was the best place for Victorio, but even his powerful voice failed to change the Indian Office's opinion.

In Alamosa Canyon, Victorio found more than a hundred of his followers who had hidden from the military when they'd come to escort the tribe back to San Carlos the previous autumn. They desperately needed food, and in October Victorio led a raiding party into Mexico for cattle and horses. During his absence, the army attacked and destroyed his camp, and among the mostly women, children, and elders killed was his first wife. Thus began what historians have come to call Victorio's War.

It lasted a year, during which time Victorio and Nana raided from Warm Springs across into west Texas and southward into Mexico. They moved constantly through different mountain ranges, frequently splitting their forces and attacking simultaneously in different areas miles apart. Ranches, farms, military patrols, and supply trains all became targets. One estimate, by a soldier who chased him during this time, estimated the marauders killed more than a thousand whites and Mexicans. This is a huge exaggeration, but many in the military did agree Victorio proved himself to be a superb guerilla fighter, better even than Cochise.

On September 11, 1879, for example, the Apache chieftain and his men ambushed an armed group of civilian volunteers searching for him near the McEvers Ranch, located between fifteen and twenty miles south of present-day Hillsboro, New Mexico. They killed ten people and stole livestock from another nearby ranch.

The Sixth Cavalry from Arizona, the Ninth Cavalry from Fort Craig, and the Tenth Cavalry from Texas could not stop him, much less capture him. On one occasion, Victorio lured four companies (more than a hundred men) of the Ninth Cavalry, primarily Black Buffalo Soldiers, into Las Animas Canyon, then shot their horses to put the soldiers on foot. Nine soldiers died in the ambush before two more companies of the Ninth arrived to rescue them. Victorio and his band escaped without a single casualty.

A week later, the Ninth met Victorio again, this time at Cuchillo Negro north of Las Animas, and again suffered casualties without dealing a serious blow in return. From there, Victorio raided Lloyd's Ranch (near present-day Nutt, New Mexico), where he and his men killed nine men searching for him and captured a wagon train. One legend says the famed gunfighter John Ringo may have been present at this two-day engagement.

By late October, Victorio had moved into the Guzman Mountains in Mexico, and the Ninth followed across the border, but gave up because of exhaustion. Two weeks later, eighteen armed Mexican civilians searching for Victorio in the Candelaria Mountains were ambushed and killed. Fifteen more men sent to rescue them were also ambushed and killed. Victorio spent the remainder of the year raiding across northern Mexico.

By January 12, he and his band had slipped through border patrols and returned to New Mexico, but this time the Ninth finally caught up with them at Percha Creek, west of Hillsboro, and this time they used artillery. Six Apaches were reported killed, but again Victorio eluded them. He went to Ojo Caliente to try to negotiate a surrender, but when that failed, he fought the Ninth Cavalry in the nearby San Mateo Mountains, killing one officer and again escaping.

Skirmishes continued like this week after week, with only the locations changing. The Caballo Mountains. The San Andres Mountains. The Rio Grande Valley. Hembrillo Basin. The Mogollon Mountains. Alma. Palomas Creek. Deming. Back into northern Mexico.

Even the Texas Rangers found themselves chasing a ghost, as Victorio seemingly slipped back and forth across the Rio Grande at will. At most, his band may have numbered 450, but only 75 to 100 were fighting warriors. As the weeks wore on, as many as four thousand American and Mexican soldiers were chasing him.

From behind his desk in Santa Fe, Colonel Hatch was as frustrated as the soldiers in the field at how easily Victorio moved. He tasked Major Albert P. Morrow of the Ninth to keep following Victorio and essentially ordered him to defeat the Apaches. Forty-nine days later, after chasing Victorio up and down the Rio Grande Valley and even into Mexico for more than 1,100 miles, it was Morrow who admitted defeat.

Victorio knew it could not continue forever. He was pursued from every direction and had lost more than three dozen of his followers in different skirmishes, including his son. He was in his mid-fifties now, and Nana was perhaps as old as seventy. Once again, he passed close to Alamosa Canyon and sent out peace feelers to the agency there as well as to the Mescalero, telling them he was willing to surrender, but this time no one answered.

In September, Victorio headed back into Mexico, hoping perhaps to reach the Sierra Madre, where he might find safety. Instead of heading directly to the mountains where he may have thought Mexican forces would be waiting to intercept him, he led his band southeastward into the desert.

No one describes this desperate move better than author Dan Thrapp in *Victorio and the Mimbres Apaches* (1974), his biography of the Apache chief: "He led an exodus from the land and places he knew into the blazing wilderness. Toward a promised land? He could not have believed that. He was getting old. Perhaps he was tired. He had whipped his pursuers, his tormentors, time without number, but their hordes were inexhaustible, and his warriors were few and becoming weary. His was an exodus to nowhere, from the land of broken hopes to the land of no hope whatever."

The end came sometime between October 14 and 15, 1880, when Mexican General Joaquin Terrazas and 350 soldiers finally intercepted Victorio at a remote watering hole named Tres Castillos. There was a shallow lake there and the Apaches had stopped to rest. Tres Castillos translates as "Three Castles" and refers to three small but separate hills located along the edge of a dry, featureless plain about ninety miles north of Chihuahua City.

The shooting began just at dusk on the fourteenth and continued periodically through the night, but ended by mid-morning after Victorio and his men had run out of ammunition. Terrazas claims he and his forces killed seventy-eight Apaches, including sixty-two warriors and sixteen women and children. Nana was not present, as Victorio had positioned him as a rear guard. Lozen, Victorio's warrior sister, also escaped, as she had remained behind during their flight to help another woman who had gone into labor.

Accounts of Victorio's death differ, even among the men of Terrazas's command, but one of the most plausible descriptions comes from an Apache named James Kaywaykla, who, in his own terms, was Nana's grandson; others believe he was Nana's great-nephew. He was ten years old and escaped from Tres Castillos with his mother during the night. They rejoined Nana, who three days afterward went to the battlefield to bury the dead.

"We found the chief with his own knife in his heart. His ammunition belt was empty," Kaywaykla told Ruidoso historian and author Eve Ball years later, recounting his conversation with Nana that Ball includes in her book, *In the Days of Victorio* (1970). "Behind rocks we found three of his men who had died by their own knives, as had Victorio. Those men we buried. We placed them beside big boulders and covered them with stones as best we could. We had nothing with which to dig."

A few survivors managed to join Nana's small band over the next several days. They dodged Mexican cavalry units searching for them, and as they approached the New Mexico border, they were forced to hide from an American cavalry unit heading into Mexico to join the search. Nana headed west and slipped into Arizona instead, hiding in the Mogollons to rest and organize his group, for he was now their acknowledged leader.

"Nana deeply and sincerely wanted peace, but he wanted his own country, his freedom, and that of his people to enjoy living in their own land," Kaywaykla relates in *In the Days of Victorio*. "His endurance seemed endless, his patience effortless. No young man in the tribe could spend more hours in the saddle without rest than he."

From the Mogollons they gradually made their way into Mexico to the Sierra Madre. There Lozen joined them, and later they united with Juh, leader of the Nednhi band of Apaches, at his stronghold on the northeast edge of the Sierra Madre. Geronimo, Juh's brother-in-law, and his band were already there.

Nana then began a phantom-like six-week-long series of retaliatory attacks and ambushes across parts of Mexico, southern New Mexico, and west Texas the following summer of 1881. He and his small group—some say he only had fifteen warriors—covered more than a thousand miles and killed more than thirty Americans. As he had done with Victorio, Nana moved with lightning speed and frequently divided his small force to be able to attack different places simultaneously. At one point they were successfully eluding nearly a thousand

Nana fought against the Mexicans and the Americans his entire life, and even after years of imprisonment in Florida and Oklahoma he was not allowed to return to New Mexico with other freed Apaches. *Ben Wittick Collection, Palace of the Governor Photo Archives, New Mexico Historical Museum*

Guarding waterholes proved to be an effective tactic against both Victorio and Geronimo. Arizona Historical Society

US cavalry and their Indian scouts. Historians have named this fierce reprisal Nana's Raid, and it ended when Nana retreated into the rugged Sierra Madre Victorio had tried to reach.

Nana surrendered to General Crook on May 23, 1883, and was sent to San Carlos. Two years later, he and Geronimo, forty-two warriors, and approximately ninety women fled the hated reservation and managed to elude capture for three more years until he surrendered one final time with Geronimo in 1886.

There were, and continue to be, many who felt sympathy for Victorio, even among those who chased him. Lieutenant Charles B. Gatewood, who would also hunt Geronimo and be the one to convince him to surrender, was quoted as saying that "any man of discretion, empowered to adjust Victorio's well-founded claims, could have prevented the bloody and disastrous outbreaks of 1879."

CHAPTER 11

THE AMERICANS: DR. MICHAEL STECK, INDIAN AGENT

Although his time in New Mexico as the Indian Agent with Victorio's Chihenne Apaches lasted only a handful of years, Dr. Michael Steck was probably the only white man Victorio ever really trusted. Three successive presidents, Millard Fillmore, Franklin Pierce, and James Buchanan, appointed Steck as an Indian agent.

Born in Hughesville, Pennsylvania, on October 6, 1818, little is recorded about Steck's childhood. Hughesville, with a population today of around 2,000, was founded in 1816 and most of the early industries there catered to area farmers. Hughesville is located in Lycoming County, approximately 130 miles northwest of Philadelphia. A nearby town, Williamsport, was once known as the "Lumber Capital of the World," so timber and logging were probably also important in the Hughesville economy during Steck's early years.

Steck graduated from Jefferson Medical College in Philadelphia in 1842 and practiced medicine in Mifflinville in Columbia County (adjacent to Lycoming County) for the next six years. He was one of fifty-nine students in his graduating class who represented sixteen states as well as Ireland and Nova Scotia. This widespread geographical diversity can be considered a testimony to the quality of instruction at the college at the time, one of the first such institutions to practice supervised, hands-on medical care. Today, Jefferson Medical College continues as Sidney Kimmel Medical College at Thomas Jefferson University and is internationally recognized for its achievements in the field of medicine.

While practicing in Mifflinville, Steck met and married Roseanna Harvey, and in 1852 the couple moved to New Mexico in hopes the dry climate there would help cure Roseanna's tuberculosis. Steck had contracted with the US Army as a physician and soon after his arrival in Santa Fe he began working with the Mescalero Apaches. Both Governor William Lane and military commander Colonel Edwin Sumner become acquainted with Steck there, and in 1853 they jointly appointed him as the temporary Indian agent for the Chiricahua. Author/historian William S. Kiser describes this appointment as one of the single most important events in the history of Apache relations with whites.

"In a world where the Apaches could trust almost nobody, they found a friend in Michael Steck," Kiser writes in *Dragoons in Apacheland*, a superbly researched book describing US Army activities against the Apaches in pre–Civil War New Mexico. "Throughout the several years in which he served as their agent, the doctor remained steadfastly dedicated to the unpopular ideology of fair, equitable treatment for the Indians of southern New Mexico. Gradually, through countless acts of kindness and forbearance, he earned the trust of nearly every chief."

Steck's willingness and his ability to communicate effectively with the Apaches certainly prevented additional bloodshed on more than one occasion. The first Indian Agent for the Apaches, Jack Hays, had been appointed in 1849 but he resigned before Victorio likely ever met him. Several others followed Hays, and they, too, hardly remained long enough to unpack their travel bags.

Agents were chosen by the Department of the Interior's Indian Office, which historically was one of the most corrupt offices in the government. These men were not hired because of any special qualifications they possessed, so virtually none were prepared for the work they faced. The Indian Office also acted very slowly on all decision-making, possibly because the Department of War, which originally controlled the Indian Office, was constantly feuding with the Interior Department about how to deal with the Indians.

Agents were responsible for a tribe's general welfare, including keeping the peace and enforcing rules, ordering and distributing food and supplies, negotiating treaties, and at times suggesting and marking potential reservation sites. Some agents took the job because they viewed it as a chance to get rich quick—there were numerous ways to divert government funding into their own pockets. The corruption extended throughout the chain of command, from agents to superintendents to governors and military leaders.

Inflating contract prices and cutting rations were common. Final budgetary approval for all expenditures lay with Congress, which like the Indian Office itself was usually slow to act. Thus, rations and supplies were habitually late to arrive—sometimes never arriving at all—and when this occurred, the Apaches could only blame the agent. They had no real understanding of a faraway government in Washington.

Steck moved from Santa Fe to Fort Webster, arriving at the dilapidated fort near Santa Rita on July 8, 1853. In early November 1854, the fort was abandoned and he moved to newly constructed Fort Thorn on the west bank of the Rio Grande, not far from the present-day town of Hatch. Victorio's Warm Springs band and the so-called Copper Mine Apaches under Mangas Coloradas had been joined as the Southern Apache Agency, and Steck was in charge of both.

The first thing Steck learned was that during his single year in office, Governor William Lane had spent all the funds allocated for purchasing rations for Steck's two Apache bands. At the same time, the new agent recognized immediately that if he asked the Apaches to give up their subsistence raiding into Mexico and establish permanent living camps, as stipulated in the Treaty of Guadalupe Hidalgo, he had to provide them rations to make up the difference. The only thing he could do was try to get the bands to start growing their own crops.

Apache efforts at planting were limited because the only cultivation tools they had were pointed sticks. The American government had never provided them with even rudimentary hoes. Still, Steck got down on his hands and knees in the dirt to show the Apaches how to plant, and this may have been how he first met Victorio.

Steck permitted the Apaches to continue hunting, but wild game was scarce during the warm New Mexico summer, and when the government finally began issuing rations the amounts were below even subsistence levels. They were forced to eat their own mules and horses, along with mescal, juniper berries, and acorns. There were subsistence raids into Sonora and Chihuahua, as well, but for the most part, Victorio and his band tried to do what Steck instructed them to do.

"Without one exception the principal chiefs seem willing to attempt the cultivation of the soil if means can be furnished to assist them," Steck wrote to Indian Commissioner George Manypenny. "They already feel their dependence upon the Govt and by the judicious expenditure of $1,000 during the present year many hundred bushels of corn can be produced principally by the labour of the Indians themselves. They can be made to see the advantages of this course and in a few years be permanently located."

Steck knew he needed to get the Apaches on a permanent reservation before encroaching Americans eliminated their hunting and before the inevitable clashes with those Americans escalated. Steck received virtually no help in this from then New Mexico Governor David Meriwether, but when Meriwether resigned in late 1857 and the Santa Rita copper mines reopened a few weeks later, Steck acted on his own.

He established a new agency on the bank of Alamosa Creek—Victorio's birthplace—and named it the Warm Springs or Ojo Caliente Agency. The valley was large enough to support Victorio's and Mangas Coloradas's bands, and even the Mescaleros, as well, Steck wrote the Indian Office in Washington. True to form, the Indian Office took its time to address the issue. In fact, they didn't reach a decision for over twenty years.

In 1860, gold was discovered in Bear Creek and the town of Birchville was established practically overnight. This eventually became the settlement of Pinos Altos. Even as miners flooded into the area, Washington refused to act on Steck's requests to formally establish the reservation at Alamosa Creek and Congress halted appropriations for rations. Discouraged and disgusted at the same time, Steck left his position as Indian agent and entered politics that same year. He ran for the position of territorial delegate to Congress from New Mexico, and was elected.

Victorio and his band of Chihenne Apaches continued to live in Alamosa Canyon, but after the Civil War started and American soldiers headed east, he joined Cochise and Mangas Coloradas and immediately began raiding across southern New Mexico, intent on driving out as many other Americans as possible. Steck returned to the Alamosa Canyon Agency during the summer of 1861 to try to restore some semblance of order, but as the rumors and threats of an invasion of New Mexico by the Confederates grew stronger, he soon left for Santa Fe.

In May 1863, Steck was appointed superintendent of Indian Affairs for New Mexico. He and General James Carleton, also headquartered in Santa Fe, clashed immediately. Some reports say Carleton even refused to talk to Steck, or did so only sparingly. The former leader of the California Column was determined to eliminate the "Indian problem" by concentrating them at Bosque Redondo, and he didn't want any interference from the Apache agent.

Carleton started with the Mescaleros in southeastern New Mexico, followed by the Navajo, but supporting two tribes on the remote outpost was expensive. The first year, he spent nearly $1 million at Bosque Redondo, and that's what Steck complained about to the Indian Office in Washington. In addition, he wrote, food there was in short supply, the Pecos River water was too alkaline to drink, and the two tribes strongly disliked living together in such close proximity.

Steck listened to Victorio's pleas to create a permanent reservation for his band in Alamosa Canyon, and in turn he pleaded with Washington to act on that request. At the same time, Steck never stopped telling the Indian Office what a mess Carleton had made of Bosque Redondo. Finally, in the fall of 1866, Carleton was relieved from duty and the reservation closed.

The continuous fight against Carleton and the Washington bureaucracy had taken its toll on Steck, however. Not long after Carleton left Bosque Redondo, he resigned his position as Superintendent of Indian Affairs in New Mexico and retired to a farm near Winchester, Virginia. He died there on October 6, 1880, just four days before Victorio and his band were killed at Tres Castillos.

He is buried at Mount Hebron Cemetery, 305 E. Boscawen Street, Winchester, Virginia.

CHAPTER 12

PLACES TO SEE: ALAMOSA CANYON, FORT CRAIG, KIT CARSON HOME

The very first things a visitor to Alamosa Canyon notices are the huge cottonwood trees growing along the lower portion of what was once Alamosa Creek. These are the trees that gave the canyon one of its several names, Canada Alamosa, and are a fitting introduction to one of the most sacred areas in Apache history. According to their oral history, this canyon is where the Apaches originated.

The canyon is also known as Warm Springs or, as the Spanish described it, Ojo Caliente, named for the constant 110-degree-Fahrenheit water coming out of natural hot springs located in the upper end of the canyon. This is believed to be the birthplace of Victorio, between 1820 and 1825, and his sister Lozen, perhaps in 1840. Throughout his later years when the American military tried to put the Apaches on reservations, Victorio lobbied desperately for a reservation that included this canyon. Even when eluding American cavalry units, he frequently returned here.

The majority of the canyon today is privately owned by the Coil family and is part of their 74 Ranch. The warm waters flowing the length of the canyon in Victorio's time are not as active as they were 150 years ago, and most of the water is diverted now for irrigation. Visitors can still drive several miles until having to turn around at a locked gate and before reaching either the narrow Alamosa Canyon Box or the hot springs. The narrow dirt/gravel road crosses the creek several times, and steep rock walls give way to higher grassy slopes where the Apaches likely camped and grazed their horses.

The road into the canyon begins in the historic village of Monticello, where Victorio and other Apaches frequently traded goods taken during raids into Sonora and Chihuahua. Today, Monticello is still a quiet, out-of-the-way village, but little if anything remains from Victorio's time. The oldest structure is probably the small Catholic church located on the main street, but no date is given for its construction.

To reach Monticello and Alamosa Canyon, follow I-25 south from Albuquerque approximately 175 miles to Exit 89 (at mile marker 90, the interstate crosses the normally dry Alamosa Creek) and follow the road signs approximately fourteen miles to Monticello, located on New Mexico Highway 142. Continue through Monticello on the main road, past the cottonwood trees and into Alamosa Canyon.

Before reaching Monticello, New Mexico Highway 52 branches to the left and offers a scenic drive to the settlements of Cuchillo, Winston, and Chloride. This was all Apache land and regularly traveled and hunted by Victorio and his band, and deer, elk, and antelope can often be seen grazing on the hillsides. Watch for cattle along Highway 52 as well, since several of the ranches along this route do not have fences along the road. Chloride was a mining town and today the local museum provides a glimpse into that era.

During much of Victorio's lifetime, roughly between 1846 and 1880, the United States military constructed some sixty forts across New Mexico, primarily to protect immigrants and shipping, and to control the Apaches. Some of these forts were hardly more than a few scattered log or adobe buildings that have long since disappeared, while others were far larger installations, several of which are still in use today. All, however, played a role in the lives of Cochise, Mangas Coloradas, Victorio, and Geronimo.

Very little remains of Fort Craig (1854–1885), one of the most important of these installations, but in 1862 it was the largest military post in the Southwest. Nearly four thousand soldiers were stationed there at that time, and their mission was not limited to fighting the Apaches. Located on the northern edge of the Camino Real, the old Spanish travel route between El Paso and Santa Fe, the soldiers were also tasked with protecting those travelers as well as the immigrants who came to

Victorio and his sister Lozen are believed to have been born in Alamosa Canyon, which may be one reason he returned to it, even when being pursued by American forces. Water still flows through the canyon and elk and deer are still present.

stay in the region to farm or raise cattle. Thus the fort, despite its isolation, was actually a small community, with a hospital, blacksmith's shop, school, and other facilities.

Both infantry and cavalry were stationed here, including the Ninth Cavalry and Thirty-Eighth and 125th Infantry units of African American Buffalo Soldiers. On February 21, 1862, Fort Craig's Union forces, including a thousand New Mexico Volunteers led by Kit Carson, engaged 2,600 invading Confederates at Valverde, a crossing spot on the Rio Grande about five miles north of the post. The Confederates drove the Union troops back to Fort Craig, but lost their supply wagons in the process.

Following the Civil War, Fort Craig's troops concentrated on the Apaches, particularly Victorio, Geronimo, and Nana. When Victorio and his warriors captured forty-six horses from Company E of the Ninth Cavalry in September 1879, another company of the Ninth went after them and soon were themselves trapped in a remote canyon by the warriors they'd been chasing. They were forced to abandon most of their own horses to escape. These were the types of clashes that dominated military activity at Fort Craig, and by the end of 1879, the entire Ninth Cavalry was pursuing the elusive Apache chieftain. Fort Craig was permanently closed in 1885, five years after Victorio's death.

Fort Craig is located thirty-five miles south of Socorro, New Mexico, on Bureau of Land Management property approximately eight miles east of I-25. When traveling south on I-25, take the San Marcial exit; if traveling north on I-25, take Exit 115. Signs point the way to the ruins, which are open year round.

The Kit Carson home, where the frontiersman and his wife Josefa lived from 1843 to 1868, is located at 113 Kit Carson Road, Taos, New Mexico, a short walk from the city's central plaza. The home was built about 1825, and was designated as a National Historic Landmark in 1963.

Built in 1854 to help protect travelers moving along the old Camino Real travel route between El Paso and Santa Fe, by 1862 Fort Craig was the largest military installation in the Southwest. Following the Civil War, troops stationed at the fort concentrated primarily on controlling Victorio and Nana.

The home serves as a museum and consists of several rooms that have been furnished in the Spanish Colonial style of that era, although few if any of the furnishings actually belonged to Carson. The walls are adobe and the floor is wood planking, while the front of the building opens into a small courtyard. Property deeds from 1850s show a well in the courtyard. The home is open daily between 10:00 a.m. and 5:30 p.m., and an admission fee is charged.

Carson and his wife are buried nearby in Kit Carson Memorial State Park. The graves are located in a corner of the cemetery, marked with an American flag.

The veteran mountain man and guide Kit Carson played an important role during the Apache Wars, bringing the Mescaleros into Bosque Redondo, even though it was not a job he wanted. His home in Taos, built in 1825, is furnished in the Spanish Colonial style of the era.

CHAPTER 13

THE APACHES: GERONIMO

It was during the season of the Little Eagles, the beginning of summer, and on the night he was born the sky blazed with shooting stars. To the Apaches, this was a powerful omen, one that meant the newborn child was a special child, one empowered with certain gifts. In the morning his father sprinkled sacred pollen over him to further emphasize the child's special gifts, whatever they might be.

The year may have been as early as 1823 but more likely was actually 1829, and the place was on the western bank of the Gila River near the headwaters where the river forks in northern New Mexico. His birth name was Guu yuu le n, but soon his father began calling his son Guu ji ya, meaning "the clever one." The baby started crawling when just a few months old, and was always exploring new places, new sights, and new sounds.

It is a warm, bright afternoon, and Harlyn Geronimo and I are sitting in the lobby of the Inn of the Mountain Gods in Ruidoso. Harlyn is describing his great-grandfather, the Apache warrior Geronimo.

"What was the sacred pollen?" I ask.

Harlyn looks at me and smiles, then points across the lake behind the Inn to a shoreline covered with cattails. "There," he says. "It is *hoddentin*, the yellow pollen from the tubers of the cattails, that is sacred to us." He, like his great-grandfather, is a medicine man for the Chiricahua Apaches and knows each of the more than three hundred sacred ceremonial plants.

He was seventy-two when we first met, slim and alert, patient and soft-spoken with outsiders like myself, and unquestionably proud of his heritage. His father was the son of Lana Geronimo, the daughter of Kate and Geronimo. Kate and Geronimo had been married several years before Geronimo's surrender in 1886, and when he was allowed to, he sent Kate and Lana back to the Mescalero Reservation, rather than remain at Fort Sill where he was imprisoned. It was Kate who taught Harlyn how to recognize and use the medicinal plants; she chose to transmit her shamanistic power to him when he was five years old.

On this particular afternoon, Harlyn was dressed comfortably in cowboy boots, pressed jeans, a light sport coat, and a white Stetson. He served two hard combat tours in Vietnam and was never wounded. His father came ashore at Omaha Beach on D-Day, and likewise never suffered a scratch. Harlyn told me that in both cases it was because of their strong Apache faith in their god, Ussen.

"What did Geronimo really look like?" I ask. "We always see pictures of him that were posed, especially the one of him kneeling with the rifle."

"According to my wife Karen's grandmother"—who was named Alberta and who lived in the Gila where Geronimo was born—"he was about six feet tall, a little taller than average but not as tall as some," says Harlyn. "He had large hands, and also broad, muscular shoulders. His hair was always cut short because his family members had been killed by the Mexicans. Among the Apaches, hair cut short like he kept his is a sign of mourning.

"He looked like he never had fear, I have been told," continues Harlyn, "and acted as if nothing was impossible. In those pictures you see, he always looks like he is mad, but I think either he did that on purpose, or the photographers asked him to. He loved children, and whenever children were present in a camp with him, they always ate first.

This posed photograph of Geronimo is one the most recognizable images of the war chief, and was taken in March 1886 by C. S. Fly at Canon de los Embudos during Geronimo's surrender talks with Crook. *Arizona Historical Society*

"He had a very deep voice, and when someone talked to him, he never blinked. He looked straight at you, like a mountain lion that is studying its potential prey."

His education as an apprentice warrior had begun about the age of eleven, by which time he was already an experienced horseman and could accurately shoot a bow and arrow, according to Harlyn. The training included being forced to run to the top of a canyon overlooking the Gila and back down, all the while holding a mouthful of water without swallowing it. By the time he was fourteen, he could stay on a horse for two days without food or sleep, and he could run all night carrying a pack.

On that particular visit, Harlyn and I talked the entire afternoon. There were some questions I asked that he politely declined to answer, because tribal tradition forbade it. I had received the same answer from Freddie Kay-dah-zinne during some of our talks. Indeed, Freddie had also told me there were certain Apache ceremonies he performed as a Chiricahua medicine man that I would not be allowed to see. Tribal traditions, almost like a type of code of conduct, are still very strong among the Apaches. If neither Harlyn nor Freddie would answer one of my questions, no one in the tribe would answer them, either.

"What I can tell you is that Geronimo was what we call a war shaman," Harlyn explained. "In our culture, every young man spends four days and nights alone on our sacred mountain praying and fasting. They have no food, water, or any type of weapon with them, only a blanket. During this time, many receive a special 'power.' It might come to them as a vision or dream, other times even as a voice speaking to them. Some do not receive any special power. Geronimo's power was both as a healer and also being able to foretell the future. As a war shaman, Geronimo said prayers before each battle and his 'power' would tell him what to do, where to place his warriors, or where to hide, even if the battle or raid would succeed.

"His instructions, or the strategy he received from these prayers, was nearly always correct. That is why he was chosen to lead in battles, and why he could elude Mexican and American soldiers so easily. His 'power' had also told him in a dream that he would never be killed in battle by arrows or bullets, and that he would be invisible to the enemy if he did not want them to see him or his warriors."

At that point, Harlyn related another story to illustrate how this "power" truly worked. It had been told to him by Lana, Geronimo's daughter and Harlyn's grandmother, who was with Geronimo when it happened. "In the late summer of 1882, they were camped on a mountainside on the Arizona-Mexico border when they saw cavalry approaching and knew there was no escape," explained Harlyn. "Geronimo began praying to his 'power,' which told him to sprinkle the sacred pollen *hoddentin* (from the cattails, which he always carried in a special pouch) on the trail the cavalry would follow. The soldiers would not be able to ride across the pollen.

"After they had done this, Geronimo led his band, including not only warriors but also many women and children, further into the hills to hide. When the cavalry reached the pollen in the trail, they simply stopped, talked for a few moments among themselves, and then the entire unit turned around and left. Geronimo and his band moved across the border into Mexico, saved once again. That is the kind of 'power' Geronimo had."

In her book *Indeh*, author Eve Ball quotes Asa Daklugie, son of the famous Nednhi Apache band chieftain Juh, and like his father also a close friend of Geronimo's, during a discussion of "power" among the Apaches. "Juh, my father, had great powers—several of them," Daklugie told her. "Like Geronimo, he could foretell the future. That is what his name means: 'he sees ahead.'

"Geronimo was by nature already a brave person, but if one knows that he will never be killed, why be afraid? I don't know that Geronimo ever told his warriors that he had supernatural protection, but they were with him in many dangerous times and saw his miraculous escapes, his cures for wounds, and the results of his medicine, so his warriors knew that Geronimo was alive only because of Ussen's protection.

"Chief Chihuahua had the 'power' over horses," continued Daklugie. "He could gentle and ride the wildest horses. He could heal them of sickness or wounds. I saw him cure a horse dying of a rattlesnake bite. And Nana—his 'power' was over ammunition trains and rattlesnakes. Long past eighty and crippled, he could ride all night and bring back ammunition for his band.

"Victorio's sister, Lozen, was famous for her 'power.' She could locate the enemy and even tell how far away it was. Many of the old Apaches today are convinced that, had she been with Victorio at Tres Castillos, there would have been no ambush."

"Does the name 'Geronimo' mean anything special?" I asked Harlyn.

"It's not an Apache word," Harlyn said, laughing. "It's the name the Mexicans gave him. Again, I have been told and also read in his biography that it happened during one of his raids and he became a recognizable warrior."

The raid Harlyn referred to could have been a fight that took place during the summer of 1859 against Mexican cavalry and infantry near the village of Arispe in Sonora, at a place known to the Apaches as Kas-ki-yeh. Here the history, and especially the dates, become confusing, since specific dates had little meaning to the Apaches. Also, at the time Geronimo spoke with biographer S. M. Barrett, he was already in his mid-seventies and his memory may have been fading.

Some believe all of this may have started several years earlier, at a place named Pozo Hediondo. The Apache attack was in revenge for an attack Mexican soldiers had previously made on a peaceful Apache camp near the village of Janos in the adjacent state of Chihuahua. During that spring (Sweeney believes it was in March 1851, not 1858), the Apaches had traveled south to trade, as they did every three to four months. The men, including Geronimo, spent the day in town trading horses, tanned deer and elk hides, and other items for food, rifles, and ammunition while their wives and children remained in camp. The Apaches never attacked Janos because of this trading arrangement, which had been continuing for years.

On this particular day, however, Mexican troops from Sonora led by Colonel Jose Maria Carrasco illegally crossed the border into Chihuahua, found the Apache camp, and killed the few warriors guarding the camp, along with most of the women and children. Then they were scalped, because the Sonoran government was paying a bounty on every Apache scalp brought in. The soldiers also took what weapons they could find, captured the band's horses, and destroyed all the food and supplies.

When Geronimo and the approximately eighty men returned from their day of trading, they were met outside the camp by the few survivors who related the grisly horror of just a few hours earlier. In the camp, Geronimo found the bodies of his mother, his wife, and their three small children. According to Sweeney, who described the Mexican leader in his book *Mangas Coloradas*, Carrasco "thought himself omniscient. Believing he was Sonora's savior, Carrasco exhibited an arrogance and driving temperament that effortlessly offended anyone who annoyed or inconvenienced him."

As darkness fell, the surviving Apaches began their long, sorrowful walk back to Arizona. Geronimo himself, according to his biographer S. M. Barrett, remembered, "I stood until all had passed, hardly knowing what I would do—I had no weapon, nor did I hardly wish to fight, neither did I contemplate recovering the bodies of my loved ones, for that was forbidden. I did not pray, nor did I resolve to do anything in particular, for I had no purpose left."

Several days later the Apaches reached their own camp, and by then Geronimo had vowed vengeance on the Mexican troopers who had murdered his family. His first opportunity came during the fight at Kas-ki-yeh the following summer. Mangas Coloradas, chief of the Bedonkohe band, had been joined by the bands of Cochise and Juh, and because Geronimo himself had lost the most family members in the Mexican assault, Mangas appointed him to guide them across the border and to lead them in the attack.

Geronimo guided the three bands on foot, traveling forty to forty-five miles a day until they came to the outskirts of Arispe and set up camp. Before long, eight Mexican riders came into the camp to parley with the Apaches. "These we captured, killed, and scalped," Geronimo remembered. "This was to draw the troops from the city, and the next day they came. The skirmishing lasted all day without a general engagement, but just at night we captured their supply train. As we had anticipated, about ten o'clock in the morning the whole Mexican force came out. I recognized the cavalry as the soldiers who had killed my people at Kas-ki-yeh."

The soldiers were lured into timber where Geronimo had concealed the warriors, and before they recognized their mistake, he led a headlong charge right into them. At the same time, other warriors attacked from the rear, in effect surrounding the troops. Only a handful are thought to have escaped. "In all the battle I thought of my murdered mother, wife, and babies . . . and my vow of vengeance, and I fought with a fury," Geronimo told Barrett. "The battle lasted about two hours. I could not call back my loved ones. I could not bring back the dead Apaches, but I could rejoice in this revenge. The Apaches had avenged the massacre of Kas-ki-yeh."

The word "Geronimo," apparently uttered by some of the Mexicans as they fought, is the Spanish form of the Greek name Hieronymos, or Jerome, and literally means "sacred name." It normally refers to St. Jerome, the Catholic priest who translated the Bible into Latin, but at the same time the name was also used as a euphemism to denote a pagan deity. Geronimo literally could have been fighting so furiously—and apparently he could not be killed—that the Mexicans may have felt they were fighting the devil himself.

Geronimo held his resentment of the Mexicans the rest of his life. He is quoted by Barrett as saying, "I have killed many Mexicans; I do not know how many, for frequently I did not count them. Some of them were not worth counting.

"It has been a long time since then, but still I have no love for the Mexicans. With me, they were always treacherous and malicious. I am old now and shall never go on the warpath again, but if I were young, and followed the warpath, it would lead into Old Mexico."

Geronimo's grandfather, Maco, a highly regarded and successful chief of the Nednhi Apaches, seemingly passed on his aggressive genes to the grandson he never knew, for he spent much of his own adult life fighting the Mexicans. He died of an illness when his own son, Geronimo's father Tak-li-shim, was still young. Tak-li-shim later married a Bedonkohe Apache, and by tribal tradition left the Nednhi to live with them. This effectively took away his right to become an hereditary chieftain, as it also did as for his own son, Geronimo. Mangas Coloradas thus became chieftain of the Bedonkohe.

Geronimo's father died when he was still a young boy, and his mother never remarried, although she certainly could have. He assumed responsibility for her, even after he was admitted into the council of warriors and allowed to participate in raids. The year was 1846 and he was seventeen years old. This was also the year he married Alope, whom he had secretly been courting for some time. Over the next several years, they had three children; this was undoubtedly the happiest time in Geronimo's life, until Colonel Carrasco and his Mexican cavalry changed it on that fateful day in Janos.

Over the next several years, Geronimo led numerous raids into Mexico, still fighting for revenge as well as for subsistence supplies, especially cattle, horses, and rifles. He had probably seen his first white men by this same time, the Boundary

Commission led by John Russell Bartlett. Bartlett, a former banker and writer, had accepted an annual salary of $3,000 plus expenses to survey the new boundary between the United States and Mexico, even though he was completely unqualified for the job. Mangas Coloradas, probably along with Geronimo, met them in mid-1851 when they reached Santa Rita del Cobre and set up temporary headquarters.

For a short time relations between the Apaches and the Boundary Commission went well, until a Mexican worker shot and killed an Apache during an argument. Soon, a few horses and mules began to disappear from the commission stables, causing tensions, as well as distrust, to rise between the Apaches and the Americans. For still another era in the entire history of the Apaches and Americans, a single event began to set the course of the future.

The Bascom Affair in 1861, at which Geronimo was not actually present, certainly added to his distrust of the Americans, as it did for all Apaches. In early 1863, when Mangas Coloradas was murdered by white soldiers at Fort McLane after he had come in seeking peace, Geronimo vowed never to be friends with the whites. He had tried to convince Mangas not to go to Fort McLane because the Americans could not be trusted, and he was proven right.

Geronimo's specific activities in the years immediately following the death of Mangas Coloradas are difficult to pinpoint with certainty, since the Apaches kept no written records. It is safe to say he led raids into Mexico, continuing his revenge against Sonora. Very likely he was joined by Juh on some of these. He also spent considerable time with Cochise and Victorio, ambushing and raiding American wagon trains, mining camps, and military patrols as part of Cochise's own vicious war of revenge stemming from the Bascom Affair. Geronimo often lived in the Dragoons with Cochise, as well as at Ojo Caliente with Victorio.

The Civil War pulled many of the American troops away from their Arizona and New Mexico posts, and Geronimo almost certainly felt as Cochise did, that they were actually driving the whites out of their homeland. When several of the forts were not only abandoned but also burned by the departing troops, this belief became even stronger. The Apaches could not understand American soldiers fighting each other on the scale of what was happening at Shiloh, Chancellorsville, or Gettysburg.

Geronimo does not spend a lot of time in his autobiography with Barrett discussing details of this particular period in his life. He does say he was elected tribal chief shortly after the death of Mangas Coloradas. Both Harlyn and Karen confirmed this to me, but many historians question it because of known Apache traditions. Geronimo also describes losing warriors, women, and children to attacking American military patrols, then taking his band to Alamosa Canyon and living quietly with Victorio for a year or more.

We do know Geronimo and his band had returned to the Dragoons by 1871 and were living with Cochise and the Chokonen, and that he was present when Tom Jeffords led General Howard into the Stronghold to make peace with Cochise in 1872. Howard clearly remembered meeting Geronimo, according to correspondence he exchanged with Barrett nearly thirty-five years later, in 1906. In fact, Geronimo rode double with the general on his horse on their way to Fort Bowie.

A year earlier, in June 1871, the man who would become Geronimo's nemesis for much of the next fifteen years, General George Crook, had arrived in Arizona. At that particular time, Crook was not necessarily well thought of by his peers, and even William Tecumseh Sherman, Grant's commanding general of the army, voiced his own dissatisfaction with the selection.

Crook was forty-two years old and only a brevet general. He was actually a lieutenant colonel, and thus when he was appointed by President Grant to command all military forces in Arizona, several higher-ranking officers were passed over for the post. Crook himself was not overly happy with this new assignment and actually refused it. He had spent years in the Pacific Northwest fighting different tribes in that region, and he has often been quoted as saying he was "tired of Indian work."

Crook was well aware of the antagonistic feelings of those higher-ranking officers Grant had ignored when making his choice, and he also knew how the Apaches essentially ruled the Arizona Territory. His job was not going to be easy, and it was only after repeated intervention by Arizona governor Anson Safford that Crook finally agreed to the command.

On his very first tour of the territory, as bands of Apaches disappeared and melted into the rocks and cliffs at his every approach, Crook made what was probably the single most important decision he could make in his future fight against Geronimo: He fired the Mexican scouts and trackers he had been using and replaced them with Apache scouts.

While on this initial foray through Apacheria, Crook also encountered then Second Lieutenant John Gregory Bourke, who remained at his side as aide-de-camp through Geronimo's final surrender in 1886. Born in Philadelphia on June 23, 1846, Bourke had run away from home in 1862 at sixteen and served as a private in the Fifteenth Pennsylvania Cavalry throughout the remaining three years of the Civil War. He received the Medal of Honor for his gallantry in action during the battle of Stone River in Tennessee on December 31, 1862, and January 1, 1863. After the war, he attended West Point, graduating eleventh in his class of thirty-nine, and was commissioned a second lieutenant. He was assigned to the Third United States Cavalry and was stationed at Fort Apache when he met Crook.

Bourke's contribution to history is that he was not only a soldier but also a keen observer of the Apaches, including their lifestyle, customs, fighting ability, and the land in which they roamed. He lived with them for a time and learned their language. More importantly, Bourke chronicled all that he saw and experienced with Crook, leaving not only accurate but also very readable historical accounts of those experiences. Two

General George Crook twice thought he had secured Geronimo's surrender, but both times the Apache war chief either escaped (from the San Carlos Reservation in 1885) or refused to come in (Canyon de los Embudos the following year). Crook usually rode a mule, rather than a horse, and rarely wore his military uniform in the field. *Arizona Historical Society.*

of his best-known books, *An Apache Campaign in the Sierra Madre*, published by Scribner's in 1886, and *On the Border With Crook*, also published by Scribner's in 1891, have long been considered to be among the most valuable references of the Apache Wars. Bourke died at the age of forty-nine, by then a colonel, on June 8, 1896, and is buried at Arlington National Cemetery.

Crook's relationship with Grant was likely strained to some extent when, in early 1872, he received news that General Oliver O. Howard would soon be arriving in the territory on a special mission as a peace commissioner and specifically to meet with Cochise, if possible. Cochise, of course, was also on Crook's list, but for a different reason. If the Chiricahua leader could not be persuaded to end his hostilities against the whites, Crook and his troops would hunt him down until they killed him.

Howard arrived in April with no such intentions. The president had given him far-reaching authority to establish new reservations for the Apaches. Because he was outranked, Crook had to support him, which he did grudgingly. Even after Tom Jeffords led Howard and his aide-de-camp, Lieutenant Joseph A. Sladen, into the Cochise Stronghold and established a reservation for the Chiricahua, Crook remained skeptical.

With his chance to pursue Cochise thus thwarted, Crook turned his attention to other Apache bands, concentrating on a region of Arizona known as the Tonto Basin. This area of central Arizona, also known today as Pleasant Valley, lies between the Mogollon Rim to the east and the Mazatzal Mountains to the west. Tonto Creek and its tributaries flow into the Salt River and modern-day Roosevelt Lake, and Arizona Highway 188 traverses the lower Tonto Basin by the lake.

In November 1872, the basin belonged to the Tonto Apaches, among the last hostile Apaches who refused to settle on any reservation, along with a non-Apache tribe named the Yavapai, whom Americans simply named the Apache-Mojaves. Crook defeated both by late December, and by April the Tonto

Campaign was officially over, as Crook returned to Camp Verde with more than two thousand prisoners.

He turned them into successful farmers. Camp Verde was renamed Fort Verde in 1879, and today the Fort Verde State Historic Park within the town of Camp Verde is considered the best preserved military post associated with General Crook.

Geronimo and his followers had been living peacefully at Ojo Caliente with Victorio's band when Crook arrived, but by early 1872 he had moved into the Dragoon Mountains to live with Cochise. He was there when Cochise met Howard and their new reservation was established. The treaty Howard made with Cochise did not forbid raiding into Mexico, so he and groups of warriors continued to strike ranches and small villages across the border.

In his autobiography, Geronimo described General Howard this way: "He always kept his word with us and treated us as brothers. We never had so good a friend among the United States officers as General Howard. We could have lived forever at peace with him. If there is any pure, honest white man in the United States army, that man is General Howard. All the Indians respect him."

That peace began to erode after Cochise died in 1874. Taza was elected chief, but Geronimo was among those who challenged his leadership. Two others who were more vocal than Geronimo, Pionsenay and his brother Eskinya, had their own group of supporters and broke away to establish their own camp. On April 7, 1876, they killed two white men, Nicholas Rogers and Orisoba O. Spence, who refused to sell them whiskey, and while some accounts list Geronimo as being part of this, his actual presence is difficult if not impossible to verify.

What is known without question is that this was one of an ongoing sequence of events that led to the closing of the Chiricahua Reservation barely a month later. John P. Clum, the Indian agent at San Carlos, was ordered south to escort the Chiricahua back with him to the dreaded reservation in the desert. Clum couldn't do that alone, so he brought along his own police force, fifty-four White Mountain Apaches, longtime antagonists of the Chiricahua.

"Geronimo and Juh both agreed to go to San Carlos with Clum," Harlyn explained to me during one of our visits, "but they told Clum that their respective bands were scattered across the reservation and even into Mexico, and they needed several weeks to gather them. This, of course, was an excuse that might allow them to get safely away, but Clum only allowed them four days. Geronimo, Juh, and the other leaders talked it over among themselves.

"The majority did not want to go to San Carlos, so that night the combined bands, possibly as many as seven hundred Apaches, slipped away. Juh returned to his hideout in the Sierra Madre, while my great-grandfather and his followers headed eastward toward Ojo Caliente where Victorio lived."

That left Clum with only 325 Chiricahua, including just sixty warriors, to march to San Carlos. By most accounts, Clum was arrogant and cocky, and he was furious at how he had been tricked. He never got over it. For as long as he was the agent at San Carlos, he tried to get even with Geronimo.

Clum's chance came in March 1877. Geronimo did move to Ojo Caliente, but he continued raiding into Mexico, virtually at will. Victorio also had trouble controlling his own young warriors who felt living off issued rations, which were frequently in short supply at Hot Springs, was too confining. Various crimes throughout the region, including the deaths of nine Americans as well as the theft of more than a hundred mules and horses, were attributed to Geronimo.

Historically, the Apaches responsible for these specific crimes have never been identified, but Clum convinced himself Geronimo was behind them all. When a military patrol recognized Geronimo at Hot Springs, Clum was ordered to arrest "the renegade Indians, seize the stolen horses in their possession; and remove the renegades to San Carlos and hold them in confinement for murder and robbery."

Clum increased his Apache police force to a hundred, and set off immediately on the four-hundred-mile trip from San Carlos to Ojo Caliente. They arrived on April 20 after three weeks of hard riding. Then, working under cover of darkness before dawn on April 21, Clum reportedly hid his heavily armed force in a cluster of buildings around the reservation office. The full details of what happened over the next several hours are still in question today well over a century later, because Clum's personal account is the only written record available.

According to him, later that morning he sent for Geronimo, who soon came in on horseback, slipped off his mount, and walked up to Clum with several of his closest followers. At his signal—Clum writes that he touched his hat—his police stepped out from hiding and surrounded the Apache leader.

"He had no choice," Harlyn related to me about this unusual moment in history, "and while he probably could have killed Clum with his knife, he himself would undoubtedly have been shot by Clum's police force. That would have left his own people without a leader and many of them undoubtedly would have also been killed. He surrendered, and along with several others, was immediately shackled and chained.

"In his biography, Geronimo himself tells very little about what happened that day, or along the journey," Harlyn continued. "He only says that he was put in a guardhouse at San Carlos and remained there for several months. Then, supposedly after a trial, he was released. Among the Apaches, we have no written record of this event, and most of us doubt it happened the way Clum reported it. I am almost certain my great-grandfather surrendered because he was thinking more about the safety of his people than about himself."

Daklugie, Juh's son, later totally denied Clum's dramatic account of how the agent took Geronimo prisoner. "If the melodramatic scene described as Mr. Clum's 'capture of Geronimo' occurred, no Apache knew of it," he told Eve Ball, "and about five hundred witnessed the event."

Victorio was also taken prisoner but apparently not shack-led. Clum's description of Victorio that day is worth noting, as it shows the contrast between himself and Geronimo. "His long black hair, tinged with gray, glistened in the morning sun. He carried his rifle resting easily in the crook of his left arm, its muzzle protruding from under the light blanket thrown carelessly over his shoulder. His serious, intelligent face was unmarred by war paint, and as he walked, his head turned slowly while he surveyed the unusual picture in front of him."

Before he and 453 Chihenne and Chiricahua began the long walk from their beloved valley to the hot, dry San Carlos Reservation on May 1, as many as two hundred may have escaped into the mountains, hiding their weapons for possible future use. Spring monsoonal rains caught the prisoners as they trudged westward over the mountains and into the Arizona des-ert, and eight died from smallpox before the procession reached San Carlos on May 20.

With Geronimo and the other prisoners still shackled securely in the reservation guardhouse, Clum bombarded his superiors from Tucson all the way to Washington with tele-grams, demanding a trial for the prisoners, a salary increase for his good work, and even funds to increase his Indian police force so he could "take care of all Apaches in Arizona" and the army would be able to remove its troops. When none of his demands materialized, Clum resigned as the Indian Agent of San Carlos. He'd submitted his resignation twice before and it had been refused, but this time the Commissioner of Indian Affairs accepted it. On July 1, 1877, less than two months after bringing in Geronimo, Clum was gone.

Not long afterward, Geronimo and the prisoners with him were released from the guardhouse, another event shrouded with still-unanswered questions. Daklugie said his father Juh confronted Clum and demanded the prisoner release, and that if Clum failed to do so, he would unite all San Carlos Apaches against him. Clum had no choice but to do as he was being told.

Geronimo himself told Barrett only that "I think I had another trial, although I was not present. In fact I do not know that I had another trial, but was told that I had, and at any rate I was released."

Things did not go as well for Victorio, however. His Chihenne were in constant conflict with the White Mountain Apaches, and on September 2 of that year, he and more than three hundred of his followers fled San Carlos and made their way back to Ojo Caliente. He surrendered to the army at Fort Wingate, who allowed the band to remain at Ojo Caliente. There they remained peaceful, contented, and relatively secure with government rations, but then, just about a year later on October 8, 1878, everything came apart again when the Department of the Interior ordered them back to San Carlos.

By month's end, the army had managed to gather 169 of Victorio's Chihenne and send them to the Arizona reservation, but the chieftain himself and perhaps as many as a hundred of his band were not among them. Realizing at last he could never fully trust the Americans, Victorio and his warriors spent the fall and winter months raiding through southwestern New Mexico. They eventually surrendered again, this time at Fort Stanton, where the agent in charge assigned them to the Mescalero Apache Reservation.

He and his band left the Mescalero in the summer of 1879 and began raiding again, this time dodging, outwitting, and outfighting literally thousands of American and Mexican infantry and cavalry until his final stand at Tres Castillos in Chihuahua.

"Geronimo and his followers did not leave San Carlos with Victorio," noted Harlyn as we watched his grandchildren playing in the lobby of the Inn of the Mountain Gods one afternoon. "They stayed at that reservation until sometime in the spring of 1878, when they broke out and headed south into the Sierra Madre. They joined forces with Juh and spent more than a year raiding in Mexico. Then, in the winter of 1879, they returned to San Carlos again and stayed until September 1881, before leaving for good."

This final departure was influenced in large part by an incident that has gone down in history as the fight at Cibecue Creek (also spelled Cibecu). The full truth of what happened August 30, 1881 on the banks of this small waterway forty-six miles north of San Carlos will never be known because, as usual, Apache accounts differ considerably from those of the US Army. Although there is no specific evidence that either Geronimo and Juh were present that day at Cibecue, a number of historians do believe they did take part.

A decade earlier, a pale-skinned, slightly built twenty-six-year-old Apache medicine man named Noch-ay-del-klinne had begun to make a name for himself among the White Mountain Apaches as a healer. In 1871 he'd been a member of a small group of Apaches who had been taken to Washington to meet President Ulysses S. Grant. Later he attended a white missionary school in Santa Fe, where he was introduced to the Christian religion. Both Cochise and Geronimo knew him.

By June 1881, the medicine man was preaching a new religion to the Apaches, a spiritual revival that mixed selected parts of his Christian study with basic Apache beliefs. He prophesied how dead warriors and chieftains would return and all white people would leave Apache land. His message included special dances and chants that continued for hours, and that the resurrection would include Cochise, Victorio, and Mangas Coloradas. Most importantly, Noch-ay-del-klinne emphasized, all of this would happen soon, by the time the corn ripened on its stalks. A number of historians have compared his message to the ghost-dance revival that would envelope the Sioux and other Plains tribes less than a decade later and eventually lead to the massacre at Wounded Knee.

As his Apache followers became more numerous and their loyalty more intense, the whites naturally grew more apprehensive, especially a man named J. C. Tiffany, the agent at San Carlos whom none of the Apaches trusted and who was later proven to be totally corrupt. Tiffany sent an urgent message to General Eugene Asa Carr, commanding general at Fort Apache, informing him of the perceived danger and essentially telling Carr he wanted the medicine man arrested, killed, or both. The general decided to lead a military force northward to Cibecue Creek, where the Prophet, as the whites had begun calling the medicine man, could be arrested.

His force included eighty-four soldiers and officers and twenty-three Apache scouts from the fort, along with an assortment of interpreters and even a number of civilians. They reached Noch-ay-del-klinne's camp on the bank of the Cibecue in a cottonwood-filled valley in the mid-afternoon of August 30. The general had sent one of his scouts ahead to tell the medicine man why they were coming, and when the troops arrived, the Prophet agreed to return with Carr to Fort Apache. At that time, about twenty Apache warriors were with the Prophet, and Carr emphasized to him that if he made any attempt to escape or if the Apaches tried to rescue him, he would be killed.

As the procession began the long ride back to Fort Apache, more and more Apaches, all heavily armed, followed. Carr selected a campsite several miles down the valley, and as the Apache scouts rode in, the shooting began. No one agrees on who shot first. An officer and two privates were killed in the first volley, and two more fell moments later as the Prophet's followers continued firing at the troops, joined by the Apache scouts. The medicine man was shot and killed by the soldiers as he tried to crawl away. The Apaches say Noch-ay-del-klinne was shot first, which is why they attacked.

The fighting continued until dark, and after burying his dead, Carr and the soldiers broke camp and started riding back to Fort Apache that same night. Many had to walk because a single Apache, thought possibly to be the warrior woman Lozen, had fearlessly ridden through the melee to stampede more than forty of their horses and pack mules. All told, Carr lost seven men and had two others wounded. The Apaches are estimated to have lost eighteen warriors, including the Prophet.

The repercussions of this short engagement were far larger than the fight itself. It was the only mutiny of Indian scouts on record, but it added more doubters to the long list of whites who argued that employing Apaches to hunt Apaches was neither useful nor safe. Virtually all of the White Mountain scouts eventually surrendered and three were executed for leading the revolt. General Carr himself, after being charged with neglect of duty and other offenses, was eventually censored, though it did little to tarnish his military career, which continued until his retirement in 1893.

Of far greater importance, Geronimo, Juh, Naiche, Cochise's son who had been serving as chieftain of the Chiricahua since his brother Taza's death five years earlier, and some seventy of their followers fled San Carlos a month later and in their own ways continued the Apache war for five more years. It started immediately. Three soldiers were killed the night they escaped. Not long afterward, as Geronimo headed southward to Juh's stronghold in the Sierra Madre, they encountered seven men leading a wagon train and killed all seven to get their supplies and horses.

David Roberts, the esteemed author of *Once They Moved Like the Wind*, writes that Geronimo's break from San Carlos "formed the fulcrum against which he drove the last five years of the Chiricahua resistance . . . his iron temper acquired a new rigor after Cibecue; his awareness of injustice hardened into a rage that lay always just beneath his implacable surface. It was during those last five years of battle that Geronimo earned the reputation as 'the worst Indian who ever lived.'"

In the Sierra Madre, however, the Apaches were not as safe from the Mexicans as in years past because their numbers had grown while the Apache numbers had dwindled. It was during a meeting of the warriors to discuss this that Geronimo proposed an audacious plan to try to even the odds: return to San Carlos where Loco, an Apache chieftain who led more than three hundred Chiricahua, Mimbreno, and Chihenne Apaches, had remained, and force them to return to the Sierra Madre. Loco had long been Victorio's second-in-command among the Chihenne (Jason Betzinez describes Loco as Victorio's co-chief, elected by the tribe), and upon Victorio's death at Tres Castillos in October the previous year, he had become the band's primary leader, with Nana serving as his backup.

The council agreed to Geronimo's plan, and a few days later he and about sixty warriors began the 260-mile trip by horseback to San Carlos. They reached the reservation in four days, completely undetected by the hundreds of American soldiers patrolling the route.

"Loco and many of the Apaches did not want to follow Geronimo because it meant more fighting, more war," explained Harlyn when I asked him about this, "but Geronimo convinced them, or maybe forced them, to join him, and so they left San Carlos. It was during this trip that Geronimo performed perhaps the best show of his 'power,' because he was able to hold back the sun for several hours."

I had read of this in my research, and now Harlyn and his wife Karen were going to explain it to me. I held my breath and waited for them to continue. "The soldiers caught up with them and there was more fighting," said Harlyn, "but that night the Apaches slipped away. They were in the mountains but before they could cross safely into Mexico they had to cross a broad, open plain, and even though it was dark, they could not make it across before dawn. The soldiers would see them and would probably kill them all.

"Geronimo told the people to continue moving out toward the open, treeless expanse, while he began praying," Harlyn continued. By now, two couples sitting at the table beside us had stopped eating and were also listening to him tell his story.

They had learned who my guests were and Harlyn was talking to them as much as to me.

"Geronimo knew dawn would come before they were safely across, but as he prayed and then rejoined his band, he also noticed the stars were not moving across the sky. That morning dawn was delayed about two hours, I have been told," concluded Harlyn. "It stayed dark long enough for the entire group, which may have been as many as four hundred men, women, and children, to cross the open plain and make it safely into the mountains on the other side.

"Today, we Apaches do not question that this happened. That is the kind of power Geronimo had, and that is what made him such a strong leader. There was more fighting before they finally reached the safety of the Sierra Madre, but they made it."

There was still one additional consequence that had its origins at Cibecue, which was President Chester A. Arthur's reassignment of General George Crook back to command the Department of Arizona, which he assumed in September 1882. He'd been reassigned from this same position in March 1875 to command the Department of the Platte, which had propelled him into the plains war with the Sioux and Cheyenne.

He'd essentially been defeated by Crazy Horse in fighting on Rosebud Creek, then missed his chance for redemption when Custer and his Seventh Cavalry rode into disaster at the Little Big Horn just eight days later. Nonetheless, he'd continued to follow and harass the Sioux throughout the autumn and bitter winter months, until Crazy Horse surrendered on May 6, 1877, not quite a full year after his greatest triumph.

From there, Crook remained on the plains, first fighting the Nez Perce, then the Bannock, the Cheyenne, and others. He'd left Arizona in relative peace, but by 1882, that peace had become a distant memory.

The Apaches had been raiding heavily in Mexico, but Crook knew new raids north of the border would soon follow. Thus, in March 1883, when a band of Apaches led by the warriors

Chihuahua and Chatto killed federal judge H. C. McComas and his wife near Lordsburg, New Mexico, and kidnapped their six-year-old son Charley, Crook was already preparing his own major offensive into Mexico.

The Apache raid lasted only six days, during which time the Indians covered some four hundred miles, killed twenty-six whites, and stole hundreds of horses. As tragic as it was, the McComas attack brought Crook one small piece of luck. One of the Apache participants, a warrior named Tso-ay (often spelled Tzoe) defected and returned to San Carlos. Because of his smooth complexion, he was named "Peaches" by the soldiers and Crook immediately enlisted him as a scout to help lead him to Geronimo.

Crook had already secured permission from Mexican officials to conduct operations in Mexico, and on May 1 he crossed into Mexico with forty-two men, six officers, and 193 Apache scouts under the command of Captain Emmet Crawford, Lieutenant Charles Gatewood, and Al Sieber. Ironically, perhaps, Crook's choice of interpreters included Mickey Free, the Mexican-Apache who as a youth was named Felix Ward, the same Felix Ward Lieutenant George Bascom had accused Cochise of kidnapping in 1861.

For the past twenty-two years, the Apaches and Americans had been fighting because of Bascom's ineptitude at Apache Pass.

Among the Apaches, Crook was known as Nantan Lupan, Chief Tan Wolf, because of his habit of wearing tan-brown civilian clothes rather than military blue. He was respected by Geronimo and the Apaches for his bravery, his fighting ability, and his fairness. He was fifty-four when he rode into Mexico that spring morning, and for the next six weeks the world would wonder what happened to them.

The route led near the town of Bavispe, then to Bacerac, and at last slightly more southeast into the ever-steeper and rougher foothills of the Sierra Madre. Everywhere, Crook could see

evidence of the Apaches moving ahead of him: trails left by stolen cattle and horses, butchered carcasses, and even saddles and
food abandoned during the climb into the mountains where no
soldier, American or Mexican, had ever dared venture. Several
of Crook's mules slipped and fell off the narrow trail.

The country "seemed to consist of a series of parallel and
very high, knife-edged hills, extremely rocky and bold . . . dense
pine forests covered the ridges near the crests . . . trails ran in
every direction," wrote Crook's aide, Bourke, in his diary of
the trip, *An Apache Campaign.* On May 10, they found the
Chiricahua stronghold, a large, grassy, pine- and oak-filled

Geronimo, on horseback, left, and Naiche, right, fought together until their
surrender in 1886. Both were imprisoned in Florida, Alabama, and Oklahoma,
but Naiche later returned to the Mescalero Reservation in New Mexico. *Arizona
Historical Society.*

amphitheater embraced by towering rock pinnacles that could easily be defended, but now it was empty. Blue hummingbirds flitted among the bushes, and Bourke found a Winchester rifle and even two children's dolls among the articles left behind.

The next day, Friday, May 11, at the request of his scouts, Crook let them move ahead to try to find the Apaches, while he and his troops remained behind to rest. They found them four days later, and even as runners brought Crook the news, distant rifle fire could be heard.

By dark, Captain Emmet Crawford, leader of one company of the Apache Scouts, and his men made it back into Crook's camp. They had engaged the followers of Bonito and Chatto, killing nine and capturing five, including Bonito's daughter. They had destroyed the Apache camp, capturing horses, meat, weapons, and other valuable supplies. The warriors had been raiding in Sonora and Chihuahua, according to Bonito's daughter, and they were stunned to see the scouts coming into their camp, particularly Peaches, whom everyone knew. Among those in the camp was the six-year-old Charley McComas, whose parents Chatto and Chihuahua had killed in March.

Over the next several days, a number of Chiricahua filtered into Crook's camp and surrendered. Among them was Chihuahua, who soon left to bring in the remainder of his followers. On May 20, less than three weeks after Crook had left Arizona, Geronimo came in. Crook spoke sparingly to him, saying only that now he could see for himself how the scouts had led the general and his force straight to their stronghold, and that Mexican soldiers were also closing in. He could make up his own mind whether he wanted war or peace.

The talks lasted on and off for several days, but Crook's terms remained stern but simple, according to Bourke. If the Apache leader was "willing to lay down his arms and go to work at farming, General Crook would allow him to go back; otherwise the best thing he could do would be to remain just where he was and fight it out," he writes. Geronimo agreed to go to San Carlos and work at farming or anything else.

Then he asked Crook to remain in camp for another week, to allow him to gather his band. Loco and the others would be back from their raiding and bring horses for all of them, especially the women and children. Geronimo was afraid if Crook left without him, the Mexican soldiers would come in and kill them all. Crook refused, but said he would travel slowly and Geronimo and his people could catch up with them.

On May 23, Nana came in with seventeen more Chiricahua, and shortly afterward Crook began the long trip back to San Carlos. Nearly 250 Apaches left with him, on foot or on mules, donkeys, and horses. Included were Loco and Nana, but not Geronimo. Crook camped after a short distance, then remained in this camp until May 28, when he again started back to Arizona. That evening, Chatto, Chihuahua, and Geronimo finally came in, leading 116 more Apaches, making a total of 384 who had surrendered. When the march renewed the following morning, the column stretched more than a mile, but again, Geronimo was not with them.

On June 15, they crossed back into Arizona and moved on to San Carlos. Three months later, Geronimo still had not come in. In October, Crook, who was taking a beating in the Arizona press for his failure to bring in the Apache leader, dispatched Lieutenant Britton Davis back to the border crossing at San Bernadino Springs to try to make contact with Geronimo or any of his followers.

"Three of the scouts were sent into Mexico as far as they dared go for fear of encountering Mexican troops but they failed to meet any of the hostiles," writes Davis in his book, *The Truth About Geronimo* (1929). "Several weeks of weary waiting followed, then one afternoon Nachite (Naiche) rode into our camp with about a dozen warriors . . . and we made quick time to San Carlos."

Buoyed by this success, Davis and his scouts returned to the San Bernadino border crossing, only to wait several more weeks. Then the sub-chiefs Chatto and Mangus, along with fifty or sixty of their followers, rode in. Again, Davis rushed them the 175 miles to San Carlos, then returned yet again to the border to await Geronimo. Six weeks later, an Apache medicine man with Davis, after hours of prayers, predicted the great warrior would arrive within three days, and that he would be riding a white horse. Virtually on cue, Geronimo rode in, bringing with him a herd of 350 cattle. When they finally did arrive at San Carlos, Crook immediately confiscated the herd.

To his credit, Crook allowed the Chiricahua to choose where they wanted to live, at either San Carlos or the adjoining Fort Apache Reservation. Unhesitatingly, the Chiricahua chose a place on Fort Apache named Turkey Creek, a grassy, pine-studded plateau overlooking Turkey Creek, a clear-running tributary of the Black River about forty miles north of San Carlos. Lieutenant Britton Davis pitched his tent among them and became close friends with a number of the Apaches.

One he never became friends with was Geronimo, who remained apart, watchful and brooding. For the next year, the Apache leader and the five hundred Chiricahua with him at San Carlos worked at becoming farmers, trying to grow corn and harvest hay in the poor soil. In August 1884, Davis had to arrest another malcontent, Kay-ten-nae, for producing and drinking tizwin, the alcoholic corn beer the Apaches had brewed for centuries, but forbidden by Crook on the reservation. Kay-ten-nae, who had never given in to reservation life, was sent to Alcatraz, at that time a prison for Indians, for eighteen months.

Tensions grew even tighter when Davis later arrested and jailed a husband who had beaten his wife, another long-standing Apache practice Crook had forbidden. Soon afterward, he jailed another who had gotten drunk on tizwin. Then Geronimo began hearing rumors that he would be tried in a civilian court for his years of raids and either imprisoned or sentenced to death.

The break came on May 17, 1885. Geronimo, Naiche, Mangus, Chihuahua—the band leaders—and their followers headed toward Mexico once again. Crook ordered several cavalry officers and their respective companies after them. Among the officers was Lieutenant Charles Gatewood, who at the time was serving as the military commandant of the White Mountain Indian Reservation, as well as overall commander of the Apache scouts at Fort Apache, just north of the San Carlos Reservation.

Gatewood had graduated from West Point in 1877 and been assigned to the Sixth US Cavalry, stationed at Fort Apache. Thus, he'd been in the Southwest more than seven years when Geronimo fled the reservation. During that time he had totally immersed himself in the Apache culture and learned to speak their language. He knew Geronimo, Naiche, and the others personally and had been part of Crook's forces during his 1883 Sierra Madre campaign. Gatewood had even been given his own Apache name, Bay-chen-daysen (Long Nose), but the lieutenant could never have imagined how his life would intertwine with Geronimo's just sixteen months later.

When Gatewood met with Crook in early June after their unsuccessful pursuit of the fleeing Apaches, he was ordered to enlist two hundred additional Apache scouts, even as Geronimo and Naiche continued to spread fear and destruction across New Mexico and Arizona from their hideouts in Mexico. There seemed to be an increased urgency in their raids, in that men, women, and children were all killed wherever they happened to be. The Apaches knew anyone left alive would tell the pursuing army where they were.

Crook sent military detachments—as many as two thousand men—to search the country from every angle, but the Apaches continued to elude them. He stationed troops at all known border crossings and waterholes, where Apache scouts searched into every nook and cranny on both sides of the line. He sent additional troops into Mexico under the leadership of Captain Emmet Crawford and Lieutenant Britton Davis.

Davis stumbled onto Geronimo's trail and with forty of the best Apache scouts followed it for more than three weeks, covering some five hundred miles of twisting turns, changes of direction, and crossing some of the roughest ground in Chihuahua. By the time they lost the trail, Davis was so exhausted and frustrated he resigned from the army and became a rancher. Then, as if to pour salt into an already open wound, Geronimo and four warriors slipped back across the border and onto the reservation to rescue his wife and three-year-old daughter.

Later that autumn, one of Geronimo's warriors named Ulzana carried out one of the most daring raids of the entire Apache Wars. David Roberts describes it best in *Once They Moved Like the Wind*: "With only ten to twelve men—fewer even than Nana had in 1881—Ulzana rode 1,200 miles in two months, killed thirty-eight, stole two hundred fifty horses and mules, and lost but a single warrior. The most daring of Ulzana's deeds came at the beginning of his wild foray, when he attacked Fort Apache itself, taking it completely by surprise."

Crook responded by sending Emmet Crawford back into Mexico, this time with a small military force but backed up with a hundred Apache scouts. They left on December 11, crossing into Sonora and establishing a base camp three weeks later at Nacori. In early January, 150 miles south of the border, the scouts found Geronimo's camp. Crawford attacked at dawn on January 10, 1886, but Geronimo and his band escaped into the mountains, leaving everything behind, including horses.

As the soldiers and scouts rested in the camp later that day, Lozen, the warrior woman who had joined Geronimo's band, approached with the message that Geronimo and Naiche wanted to talk the next day, January 11. That morning, however, Crawford's camp was mistakenly attacked by 150 Mexicans also searching for Geronimo. Crawford was mortally wounded before the shooting stopped and died seven days later. Today, more than 135 years after this engagement, details of the fight are still unclear. Lieutenant Marion P. Maus took command, and within a few days met with Geronimo. Nana and several others, including Geronimo's wife, surrendered on the spot, while Geronimo himself agreed to meet with Crook in about sixty days. During that time, Maus camped along the border to wait for some word from the Apache leader.

It came via smoke signals. Geronimo would meet Crook on March 25, at a place named Canyon de los Embudos, located some twenty miles south of the Arizona border. They met under a forest of "sycamores, ash, cottonwoods, and willows," wrote Bourke, who transcribed the verbal exchanges verbatim while a photographer named C. S. Fly, the owner of Fly's Studio not far from the O.K. Corral in Tombstone, recorded the event. This is where the famous image of Crook wearing a white pith helmet, sitting on a log with his aides across from Geronimo, Naiche, and the Apaches, was taken.

Crook listened to Geronimo, but once again took a firm, unbending stand, telling the Apache he had two choices: either surrender unconditionally, or fight it out. Geronimo was nervous, agitated, and mad. He had not expected the Nantan to treat him with so little respect. The meeting broke up and did not resume until the afternoon of the twenty-seventh. Chihuahua and his followers surrendered. Then Naiche and his group. Lastly, Geronimo and the remaining Apaches. "Crueler features were never cut," wrote an observer of the great warrior at the site. "The nose is broad and heavy, the forehead low and wrinkled, the chin full and strong, the eyes like two bits of obsidian with a light behind them . . ."

"This should have ended the last Apache war," writes Louis Kraft, the scholar who compiled and edited Lieutenant Charles Gatewood's writings into the remarkable book *Lt. Charles Gatewood & His Apache Wars Memoir* (2005). "Should have, but did not for two reasons. First, Crook's harsh attitude ate at some of the Apaches' psyche and undermined the peace talks. And second, per General Sheridan: 'The President cannot assent to the surrender of the hostiles on the terms of their imprisonment east for two years with the understanding of their return to the reservation. He instructs you to enter again into negotiations on the terms of their unconditional surrender, only sparing their lives . . .'"

That night, in the Apache camp, probably several miles from Crook's, a post trader named Godfrey Tribolet sold the Apaches enough mescal to send them all, Geronimo and Naiche included, into a drunken stupor. Crook packed up and on March 28 headed quickly back to Fort Bowie, convinced he had ended the war. Lieutenant Maus and the scouts followed with Geronimo and the other fugitives, but progressed only a few miles before making camp again.

The next evening Tribolet sold them more whiskey, and in the black of night, Geronimo, Naiche, and thirty-four men, women, and children slipped away once again. Maus, discovering Geronimo's escape the next morning, immediately set out after them with his scouts. Geronimo and Naiche's party included eighteen warriors, thirteen women, and six children, and despite having only two horses and a mule, had covered sixty miles when Maus gave up after two days.

Two days later, on April 1, Crook asked to be relieved of duty as commander of the Department of Arizona, and Sheridan, commander-in-chief of the army, accepted the resignation under President Grover Cleveland's orders. A week later, General Nelson A. Miles assumed command. Geronimo's escape effectively cancelled the surrender agreement Crook had presented at Canyon de los Embudos—two years of exile in the east, then being able to return to the reservation—but Crook never told those Apaches who had surrendered. On April 7, seventy-seven Chiricahuas were herded on board a Southern Pacific train and sent to Fort Marion, Florida. It would be twenty-seven years before any of them saw New Mexico again.

Geronimo and Naiche split the fugitive band, with Geronimo taking only six warriors and four women with him, and for more than two months this tiny group rampaged through New Mexico after easily slipping through Miles's blockade along the border. No one was safe, as ranchers, sheep herders, freighters, and virtually anyone else who was unlucky enough to be in their way was slain. The Apaches were after cattle to eat, or ammunition that would allow them to continue raiding.

The killing spree continued after Geronimo slipped back into Mexico and rejoined Naiche's band. The first thing Miles had done was end the use of Crook's Apache scouts and replace them with two thousand additional cavalry, so that he now had as many as five thousand soldiers looking for thirty-seven Apaches. The general put Captain Henry W. Lawton in charge of chasing the elusive band into Mexico with forty-five hand-picked men and a small contingent of Apache scouts, while he himself stayed in Arizona; in fact, Miles never ventured into Mexico during this time.

Lawton and his troops covered more than 3,000 miles over the next several months, during which time they found the Apaches one time, capturing some camp goods but failing to kill or capture a single member of the band. During their five-month reign of terror, the Apaches lost only three, including a woman killed by Mexicans and a warrior who left the band and gave himself up at Fort Apache. Some 3,000 Mexican troops joined in the search, making a total of more than 8,000 military personnel chasing thirty-four men, women, and children.

Apparently, Miles finally recognized the complete failure of his efforts, for on July 13, 1886, he summoned Lieutenant Charles Gatewood into his office in Albuquerque and ordered the officer to find Geronimo and Naiche. Because of his frail health, Crook had reassigned the lieutenant to Fort Wingate with orders to organize a company of Navajo scouts, but a lack of weapons had kept him from going into the field.

Miles wanted the lieutenant to take twenty-five cavalry with him, but he did not. Instead, Gatewood left Fort Bowie on July 16 with only two Apache scouts, Ka-teah and Martine, both related to members in Geronimo's band; a translator named George Wratten who spoke several Apache dialects fluently; and a mule packer named Frank Huston.

They found Lawton on August 3. The captain, physically exhausted from months of fruitless wandering in the Sierra Madre, accepted him into his command reluctantly, because he himself still wanted the accolades that would follow if his soldiers somehow engaged and killed the Apache war chief. So far, they had now been after Geronimo some four months and still had no idea where he and his band were hiding.

Then, unexpectedly, word reached them on August 19 that Geronimo had been seen just south of the town of Fronteras in Sonora, well over a hundred miles northwest of where Lawton had been searching. Gatewood and his small group of scouts and interpreters made a forced ride to the area, picked up the Apache trail, and cautiously followed it, using a white flour sack tied to the long stalk of a century plant as a sign of their peaceful intentions.

Martine and Ka-teah, moving ahead of Gatewood, returned to their camp late in the evening of the twenty-fourth. They had made it into Geronimo's camp just four miles away without being killed and delivered Gatewood's message. Geronimo, it turns out, had known of their presence for several days and sent Martine back with a lump of cooked mescal and the message that Gatewood was welcome in their camp. Naiche also added that Bay-chen-daysen should have no fear of harm from them because they trusted him.

As Gatewood and two scouts moved up the canyon toward Geronimo's camp, they were met by three armed Chiricahua warriors who directed them to a bend in the Bavispe River not far away where there was not only water, but also shade as well as grass for the horses.

Gatewood describes meeting Geronimo at the prescribed location: "Geronimo appeared through the canebrake about twenty feet from where I was sitting, laid his Winchester rifle down, & came forward offering his hand & repeating their salutation, '*Anzhoo*,' meaning 'How are you? Am glad to see you.' [We] shook hands. He remarked about my thinness & apparent bad health and what was the matter with me . . . [he took] a seat alongside [me] as close as he could get."

Thus began a meeting every bit as momentous and historic as the one between Cochise and General Howard more than two decades earlier. Gatewood and his five interpreters and scouts were surrounded by twenty-four armed Apache warriors and fourteen women and children. They combined what food they had and ate breakfast together. Gatewood passed around tobacco and necessary papers to roll cigarettes. Then the serious talk began.

Through his interpreters (Gatewood could speak the Apache language but did not trust himself to tell his simple message with absolute accuracy) he delivered the terms Miles had given him: "Surrender, & you will be sent to join the rest of your people in Florida, there to await the decision of the President of the United States as to your final disposition. Accept these terms, or fight it out to the bitter end."

Geronimo countered. They would leave the warpath only if they could return to the reservation, occupy their previous farms, and be furnished rations, clothing, and the necessary farming tools and seeds to grow their crops.

"If I was authorized to accede to these modest propositions, the war might be considered at an end right there," Gatewood writes in his memoirs, but since he was not authorized to change his proposition, the Apaches would have to change theirs. He added that this would probably be their last chance to surrender. They talked back and forth like this for an hour or two, then Geronimo and his band withdrew and talked among themselves for another hour or so.

It was noon when they resumed, and after another meal, Geronimo spoke first. Writes Gatewood, Geronimo gave his ultimatum: "Take us to the reservation, or fight." Gatewood could do neither, so he gambled. He knew Miles was planning to send all the remaining Apaches on the reservation—between four and five hundred of them—to Florida, but it hadn't happened yet. These were the wives, children, and relatives they wanted to be with on the reservation. Gatewood told them that the remaining Apaches had already been sent to Florida.

The Apaches were stunned and retired again into private conference. The two sides talked back and forth all afternoon, then Geronimo made a strange request to Gatewood that shows the depth of trust and respect they had for him. "Consider yourself one of us & not a white man," writes Gatewood. "Remember all that has been said today, & as an Apache, what would you advise us to do under the circumstances. Should [we] surrender, or should [we] fight it out?"

The small band of fugitives listened solemnly to Gatewood's reply. "[I]t was only for their good that I must council peace on the terms offered." Geronimo took the band up to their mountain camp to hold another council, telling Gatewood he would have his answer in the morning. They all shook hands firmly, and Gatewood retired to his camp to brief Captain Lawton, who had arrived there during the day.

The following morning, August 28, Geronimo and his band agreed to meet General Miles at Skeleton Canyon, located in southwestern Arizona on the edge of the Peloncillo Mountains just across the state line from New Mexico. They arrived on the afternoon of September 2. Miles rode in the following afternoon.

The Apaches crowded around the general, anxious to meet him. He told them on the reservation in Florida they would be reunited with their families who were already there waiting for them, that they would have horses and cattle, and that the land would be rich and easy to grow crops in, and that the reservation would have plenty of game. None of it was true, but now, with Geronimo and Naiche in custody because they believed him, the Apache Wars were over.

CHAPTER 14

THE AMERICANS: GENERAL GEORGE CROOK

General George Crook's reassignment to the Department of the Platte in April 1886 ended his time in Arizona and New Mexico, but it did not end his involvement in the Apache Wars. He was considered America's best and most successful Indian fighter, but for much of his career he had been tormented by two opposing ideologies. He did his best to destroy the Apache culture while at the same time harboring a growing sympathy for the very victims he created from that destruction. Eventually he became one of their staunchest allies for basic human rights.

These feelings became known publicly soon after his reassignment when his successor, General Nelson Miles, sent the Apache scouts who had aided Crook and Gatewood so diligently in finding Geronimo and Naiche, including Martine and Ka-teah, to exile in Florida. Crook had never thought much of Miles (nor Miles of Crook) from the beginning, and he spoke out publicly against the government's—and Miles's—Indian policies. He was also frustrated that Miles received the credit for obtaining Geronimo's final surrender, even though he had had almost nothing to do with it, and that Miles had lied to the Apache leader about the terms of surrender.

Lieutenant Charles Gatewood, the officer who convinced Geronimo and his band to give themselves up, was essentially forgotten by Miles. Miles had seemingly also forgotten that in the more than five months since he had taken over in Arizona, he had accomplished nothing, even with five thousand troops at his disposal. Calling everything Crook had done a "dead failure," he was finally forced to employ the very Apache scouts Crook had used.

There was little in Crook's early life to indicate the type of military giant he would become. Born on September 28, 1828 in Taylorsville, Ohio, the ninth of ten children, George Crook grew up in a quiet, hardworking, but successful farming family. "In the crowd at the Crooks' dinner table, George gave no early hint of distinction," writes Peter Aleshire in his paired biography of Crook and Geronimo, *The Fox and the Whirlwind* (2000). "He seemed painfully shy, strikingly silent. Careful, slow, and self-contained, he observed the bafflement of the world about him with an owlish detachment and restraint."

He secured an appointment to West Point through a local congressman who was looking for candidates to nominate, and in June 1849 he graduated thirty-eighth out of his class of forty-three. Although not distinguished academically, Crook had distinguished himself to his classmates by the very characteristics he would maintain the rest of his life. He was calm and remote but confident and mature, modest but stern, the same way he would later act with the Apaches.

His first assignments as a young officer took him to California and then into the Pacific Northwest where, during a decade of campaigns against various Indian tribes fighting to keep their land and their way of life in the face of incoming hordes of prospectors and settlers, he learned many of the lessons he would use later against Geronimo and the Apaches.

His disillusionment with the military leadership and mindset at these far-flung outposts began there in the Northwest, and many historians believe this is when Crook began to develop a certain sympathy, compassion, and sense of fairness for the very tribes he was ordered to subdue. Crook apparently realized during these years that the Indians were fighting to preserve their entire culture and their homeland, not just their lives, against white encroachment.

The disillusionment and disgust at the ineptitude of his commanders continued to plague Crook during his Civil War years. Attached as a brigade commander to the Army of the Potomac under Generals George McClellan and later Ambrose Burnside, he participated in some of the fiercest fighting of the entire war at Antietam, Sharpsburg, and Fredericksburg, where he witnessed the needless slaughter of thousands of Union troops because of poor decisions and squandered tactical advantages. Crook was correct in his leadership assessments, as President Abraham Lincoln removed McClellan after Antietam, and his replacement, Burnside, asked to be relieved after suffering twelve thousand casualties at Fredericksburg later that same year.

After Gettysburg, General Ulysses S. Grant was appointed the overall commander of all Union forces, and it may have saved Crook's military career. Grant certainly saved Crook's career, and very well may have saved his life, when Crook and General Benjamin Kelley were captured by Confederate soldiers in February 1865 in Cumberland, Maryland, and taken immediately to Richmond. Grant negotiated a large prisoner exchange for both men, which might not have been accomplished had it not been so near the end of the war.

"Grant and Crook shared many characteristics," writes Aleshire. "They were both rumpled, unimpressive-looking men who eschewed ceremony but who operated from a core of quiet, unshakable determination. They were both relatively remote and uncommunicative, but dogged, persistent, and relentless in seeking and exploiting the weaknesses of their enemies . . . throughout his career, Crook remained a remote figure—easy to respect but hard to like."

In part because of these shared characteristics, Grant supported Crook for the remainder of his military career. That

General George Crook spent years trying to capture Geronimo, but never succeeded. In later years, he became a strong advocate for better treatment for the Indians, and helped convince the government to end the Apache exile in Florida. *Credit: Brady-Handy Collection, Library of Congress*

was why, as President of the United States in 1871, he named Crook as commander of the Department of Arizona. With his success there, particularly in the Tonto Basin campaign, he was the natural choice to return to Arizona in 1882.

Geronimo's breakout from San Carlos in May 1885 brought bitter, unceasing public criticism to Crook. Certainly, he was as frustrated as anyone in Arizona, but he did not try to retaliate verbally. The end really came when neither President Grover Cleveland nor Phil Sheridan, commanding general of the army, agreed to the peace terms he had made with Geronimo at Canyon de los Embudos in March 1886. Crook received a telegram at Fort Bowie from Sheridan informing him of Cleveland's disapproval of the surrender even before he knew Geronimo, Naiche, and their tiny band had again escaped.

In his second assignment as commander of the Department of the Platte, which continued from 1886 to 1888, Crook spent some time dealing with the Utes, and in the spring of 1888, he was promoted to major general and assigned to command the Division of the Missouri. This included not only the Department of the Platte but also the Departments of Missouri, Dakota, and Texas; it was the largest command in the army at that time, with more than thirteen thousand men on duty.

In early January 1890, Crook visited Mount Vernon Barracks, but refused to spend any time listening to or speaking with Geronimo. He did, however, listen to other Apaches who described life in the wretched camp, and following his visit he strongly recommended to Washington that a reservation in Oklahoma be established for the remaining Apaches. Unfortunately, he did not live to see it happen.

Only a few weeks later, on March 21, 1890, he died at his home while still advocating better treatment for his former Indian adversaries. He is buried in Arlington National Cemetery, and although he has been honored many times through the years with mountains, counties, and even cities named after him, his legacy was summed up best by Red Cloud, chief of the Oglala Lakota Sioux, who said simply but succinctly, "He, at least, never lied to us. His words gave us hope."

CHAPTER 15

PLACES TO SEE: GERONIMO'S GRAVE, APACHE CEMETERIES

Approximately three hundred Apaches, including a number of chieftains and their families, are buried in three Apache POW cemeteries along Elgin Road on Fort Sill in Lawton, Oklahoma. Included are the graves of Geronimo, Chihuahua, Loco, and Nana, as well as relatives of Mangas Coloradas, Victorio, Cochise, and Naiche. Ish-Keh, the widow of Juh, is also buried here.

Beef Creek Cemetery is the largest of these cemeteries and is where Geronimo's grave can be found. It lies between two cedar trees and is marked by a mound of cannonballs topped by a silver eagle. There is no inscription, only his name, along with a few coins and feathers that have been placed in cracks around the cannonballs.

Slightly to the front and left is the grave of Eva, his daughter, and to the right is Zi-Yea, one of his wives. His son Fenton lies nearby. Nana, variously honored in military literature as the "original guerrilla fighter" or the "original desert fox," is also buried here, closer to the creek but almost in line in front of Geronimo's grave.

Overall, Beef Creek Cemetery is a sad but not really a melancholy area, located among the oak trees and easy to miss when the roadside grass is high. Literally, history lies here at

every step. These are the graves of a people who fought to preserve their land, their customs, even their language, and were
overcome only by the sheer numbers of their enemies. So much
of what could have been learned from them is now lost forever.

There is no traditional wrought iron fence or gate to separate
the cemetery from the surrounding terrain, only a plain gravel
road along one edge where visitors can park. With the exception of Geronimo's grave, each burial is marked by an identical
white military-style headstone bearing the name of the Apache
and sometimes a brief identifying inscription and the dates of
birth and death. Many of the headstones mark the graves of
young children.

It is also frustrating to think Geronimo's grave may have been
desecrated and robbed by four members of Yale University's
Skull and Bones Society in 1918. Author Mike Leach, in his
revealing book *Geronimo* (2014), writes that among the four
was Prescott Bush, the father of George H. W. Bush and grandfather of George W. Bush.

Various documents from Yale, including a letter published in
the *Yale Alumni Magazine* in 2006 as well as material Harlyn
Geronimo has himself collected, seem to indicate the story may
well be true. In 2009 Harlyn, through former attorney general Ramsey Clark, sued the university in federal district court
to have Geronimo's remains returned to the headwaters of the
Gila River for a proper burial. Also named as a defendant was
then president Barack Obama, as well as several others.

Not surprisingly, the lawsuit was dismissed on technicali-
ties, but Clark was quoted, when asked if he thought the secret
society did have Geronimo's skull and bones, said "We don't
know. There's been enough commentary about it over enough
time that you can't ignore it."

A quarter mile north of the Beef Creek Cemetery is the
Chief Chihuahua Apache P.O.W. Cemetery, dedicated to the
Chiricahua leader and his descendants. There are twenty-six
similar white headstones in this small clearing nestled in a thick

Geronimo died in 1909 in his mid-eighties and is buried in the Apache Cemetery at Fort Sill. The two smaller headstones in front mark the graves of Zi-Yea, one of his wives, and Eva, a daughter. Also buried nearby are Nana, Chihuahua, and Loco.

oak forest, including that of Chief Chihuahua, located in a back corner at the end of a line of white headstones. His inscription reads simply "Chiricahua Apache 1821 1902." His daughter, Emily Tee, is buried beside him, and Ol-Sanny, his brother, is buried next to her.

Visitors to Fort Sill need a pass to enter the post, and this can be obtained at the Visitor Control Center on Sheridan Road just before reaching the Bentley Gate. There is no charge for the Visitor Pass. Visitors can sometimes apply online for a Visitor Pass, but the system is not always working, so it is best to telephone the center at (580) 442–9603 for specific instructions.

All persons sixteen or older, even in the same family, must obtain a pass, and a valid driver's license is all the identification required. When calling, also inquire about the current hours of operation.

Personnel at the Visitor Control Center have maps of the post and can provide directions to Geronimo's grave and the Beef Creek Apache Cemetery.

EPILOGUE

When Geronimo, Naiche, Lozen, and the other Apaches boarded the train to begin their exile in Florida, many thought they would soon be reunited with their families and resettled on the green, game-filled reservation Miles had promised them. Others were apprehensive, believing they were all going to be shot once the train left Fort Bowie.

The feeling of doom only intensified when the train stopped in San Antonio, Texas, and remained there six weeks. It took President Grover Cleveland that long to decide what to do with all the Apaches. Miles had already rounded up everyone else—more than 430 Chiricahua—at San Carlos and Fort Apache and this earlier train was ahead of Geronimo's; for some reason, none of these details had been worked out in advance.

Cleveland decided the Apache women and children would be sent to Fort Marion, not far from San Augustine, but Geronimo and his warriors, who were still considered extremely dangerous, would be sent to Fort Pickens, located 350 miles across the state on an island off the coast of Pensacola. In both places, but especially at Fort Marion, the humid climate and malaria-carrying mosquitoes quickly began taking their toll on the captives.

Then, what little remained of the family units at Fort Marion were separated again. All the children between the ages of twelve and twenty-two were sent to the Carlisle Indian School in Carlisle, Pennsylvania. Among those sent was Juh's son "Ace" (the name given him at Carlisle) Daklugie and "Jason" Betzinez, a cousin of Geronimo, both of whom became important spokes-men for the Apaches in later years. Carlisle was hardly any safer than Fort Marion, however, for instead of malaria, many of the youngsters contracted tuberculosis and more than two dozen died.

Daklugie, who spent twelve years at Carlisle, described his first full day at the school to Eve Ball in *Indeh*: "The first thing they did was cut our hair. I had taken my knife from one of my long braids and wrapped it in my blankets, so I didn't lose it. But I lost my hair . . . While we were bathing, our breechclouts were taken, and we were ordered to put on trousers. We'd lost our hair and we'd lost our clothes; with the two we'd lost our identity as Indians. Greater punishment could hardly have been devised . . .

"We liked the outdoor games and contests. We liked the gymnasium, too. And the band. Of course every Apache could beat a drum, but not with two sticks as they did at Carlisle.

"Learning English wasn't too bad. There was a necessity for memorizing everything because we could neither read nor write."

The following year, the women and those children still at Fort Marion were transferred to Mount Vernon Barracks, located along the Mobile River north of Mobile, Alabama. Children returning from Carlisle brought tuberculosis with them and began to infect the adults at Mount Vernon, including Lozen, Victorio's warrior sister.

"I went to Mount Vernon Barracks and walked through the pine woods and swamps, just to see if there were any actual grave markers," Freddie Kay-dah-zinne told me during one of our interviews, "but there were none, just old mounds of dirt grown over with weeds so they were barely noticeable. This is where the Apaches buried their dead, so all we know is Lozen was buried out there somewhere.

"I was told she caught the 'coughing sickness,' as we named tuberculosis then, while she was trying to help others who already had it."

Geronimo and those who had been with him at Fort Pickens were finally transferred to Mount Vernon in May 1888, where they remained until October 1894. That year, eight years after being packed on trains and sent east, the remaining Apaches were resettled on Fort Sill in Oklahoma, on the outskirts of the present-day city of Lawton. There they remained for nineteen more years until 1913, when they were freed. They had been prisoners of war for twenty-seven years, and only 261 Chiricahua were still alive.

But they were not allowed to return to Arizona, only as far as the Mescalero Apache Reservation in New Mexico. All

Geronimo and his band await their fate prior to boarding the train that will take them to exile in Florida. Geronimo is fourth from left in the front row. *Arizona Historical Society.*

Fort Sill Apaches over the age of eighteen were able to choose whether they wanted to move or remain there in Oklahoma. Jason Betzinez writes that 127 chose to live with the Mescalero and eighty-seven decided to remain in Oklahoma. Among those who went to New Mexico were Naiche, Chatto, Daklugie, and the guides Martine and Kay-i-tah. Geronimo and Nana, both somehow still considered to be dangerous, were kept at Fort Sill.

Nana, the crippled warrior who had fought with Victorio as well as Geronimo, never accepted white society. He died in 1894 and is buried at Fort Sill. Geronimo outlived him by more than a decade, dying of pneumonia on February 17, 1909, at the age of about eighty-five. Both he and Nana are among those buried in the Beef Creek Apache Cemetery at Fort Sill. Neither man ever forgave Miles for lying to them and tricking them into surrender.

Daklugie, who was holding Geronimo's hand when he died, knew the great Apache war shaman regretted not having stayed in Mexico and fighting until the end.

ACKNOWLEDGMENTS

Writing history books always involves a number of individuals whose past research, personal involvement, specialized discipline, or just plain encouragement makes them invaluable to an author. While writing *Riding with Cochise*, I depended on many of these types of people and owe them all a large debt of gratitude.

Without question, this book would not have been possible without the help and guidance of Freddie Kay-dah-zinne and Harlyn Geronimo, who together opened a door into history I had never imagined would have still existed. Before Freddie and I met, my basic idea for this book was to write a travel guide describing prominent places of interest from the Apache Wars in New Mexico and Arizona. To better understand why the fighting had lasted so long, I needed to know more about the cultural history and lifestyle of the Apaches, and Freddie had been referred to me as the director of the Cultural Center on the Mescalero Reservation.

Early in our first conversation at the center after I learned of Freddie's direct lineage to Cochise, I stopped asking questions and just turned on the tape recorder and listened, completely in awe of the man sitting beside me and what he was telling me.

That is how our friendship began. In the months to come, we spent many, many hours together, sometimes in serious conversation but just as often not even thinking about this book. I called him any number of times at home asking for the Apache word or phrase to describe something I'd been writing about.

During our lunch breaks we talked about the food, the weather, horses, elk hunting, his children—anything and everything.

When he introduced me to Harlyn Geronimo, my door into Apache history opened wider. Harlyn was as gracious and giving as Freddie, and we subsequently also spent many hours visiting and interviewing together. The insight of these two men throughout months of interviews, their gentle suggestions for corrections and additions as this book began to take shape, and their personal friendship will always be part of my life.

A number of scholars have studied Apache history in greater detail than I can ever hope to do, and I read and reread their works carefully throughout my own writing. Among them, Eve Ball, Dan L. Thrapp, and Edwin R. Sweeney provided a line of continuity through the decades of Apache leadership that filled in some of the gaps. So did the personal journals of several of the participants themselves, particularly those of Captains Joseph A. Sladen and John G. Bourke, and Lieutenant Charles Gatewood.

Ms. Perri Pyle of the Arizona Historical Society, Ms. Catie Carl, Digital Imaging Archivist of the New Mexico Historical Museum, and staff members of the Huntington Library in San Marino, California, provided all the support any writer could want when requesting digital scans of historical photographs all more than a century and a half old. When I could not find a specific identifying number and could only give a basic description of the image I wanted, these librarians searched until they found it for me.

Writing is often described as a lonely job, and my deepest appreciation goes to my friend John Walker, who was more than ready to saddle his horse Concho and head into the mountains with me to look for a fort, a campground, or a battle site whenever I grew tired of looking at a computer screen. Ken Steinnerd, a history buff and neighbor when I lived in New Mexico, likewise kept encouraging me to continue, if for no other reason than he said he wanted to read the finished book!

Ken was with me the first time I met Freddie Kay-dah-zinne, and it was as memorable for him as it was for me.

Finally, I want to thank my wife Ann, who explored the Cochise Stronghold and walked Apache Pass with me, then for months patiently accepted the piles of reference material on my office floor, my hours of computer writing, and still diligently served as my first editor as each page of manuscript came out of the printer.

BIBLIOGRAPHY

Aleshire, Peter, *The Fox and the Whirlwind*, Edison, NJ: Castle Books, 2005.

Aleshire, Peter, *Warrior Woman*, New York: St. Martin's Press, 2001.

Ball, Eve, *In the Days of Victorio*, University of Arizona Press, Tucson, 1970.

Ball, Eve, *Indeh*, Provo, UT: Brigham Young University Press, 1980.

Betzinez, Jason, *I Fought with Geronimo*, Harrisburg, PA: Stackpole Company, 1959.

Bourke, John G., *An Apache Campaign*, New York: Charles Scribner's Sons, 1958.

Bourke, John G., *On the Border With Crook*, New York: Charles Scribner's Sons, 1891.

Carmony, Neil B. (Editor), *Apache Days & Tombstone Nights, John Clum's Autobiography 1877–1887*, Silver City, NM: High-Lonesome Books, 1997.

Chamberlain, Kathleen P., *Victorio, Apache Warrior and Chief*, Norman: University of Oklahoma Press, 2007.

Clavin, Tom, *Tombstone*, New York: St. Martin's Press, 2020.

Cozzens, Peter, *The Earth Is Weeping*, New York: Alfred A. Knopf, 2016.

Dary, David, *The Santa Fe Trail*, New York: Alfred A. Knopf, 2000.

Davis, Britton, *The Truth About Geronimo*, New Haven, CT: Yale University Press, 1929.

Davis, William C., *The Battlefields of the Civil War*, London: Salamander Books, 1990.

Drury, Bob, and Clavin, Tom, *The Heart of Everything That Is*, New York: Simon & Schuster, 2013.

Gatewood, Lt. Charles B., *His Apache Wars Memoir*, Lincoln: University of Nebraska Press, 2005.

Geronimo, Harlyn and Sombrun, Corine, *In Geronimo's Footsteps*, New York: Arcade, 2008.

Hocking, Doug, *Tom Jeffords, Friend of Cochise*, Guilford, CT: Rowan & Littlefield, 2017.

Hutton, Paul Andrew, *The Apache Wars*, New York: Crown Publishing, 2016.

Kennedy, Frances H., *American Indian Places*, New York: Houghton Mifflin Co., 2008.

Kiser, William S., *Dragoons in Apacheland*, Norman: University of Oklahoma Press, 2013.

Leach, Mike, and Levy, Buddy, *Geronimo, Leadership Strategies of an American Warrior*, New York: Gallery Books, 2014.

Lockwood, Frank C., *The Apache Indians*, Lincoln: University of Nebraska Press, 1938.

McAulay, John D., *Carbines of the US Cavalry 1861–1905*, Lincoln, RI: Andrew Mowbray Publishers, 1996.

Michino, Gregory F., *Encyclopedia of Indian Wars*, Missoula, MT: Mountain Press, 2003.

Mort, Terry, *The Wrath of Cochise*, New York: Pegasus Books, 2013.

Pattie, James O., *Personal Narrative*, Missoula, MT: Mountain Press, 1988.

Quaife, Milo Milton, *Kit Carson's Autobiography*, Lincoln: University of Nebraska Press, 1966.

Roberts, David, *Once They Moved Like the Wind*, New York: Simon & Schuster, 1993.

Sando, Joe S., *Pueblo Nations*, Santa Fe, NM: Clear Light Publishers, 1992.

Sides, Hampton, *Blood and Thunder*, New York: Doubleday, 2006.

Simmons, Marc, *Spanish Pathways*, Albuquerque: University of New Mexico Press, 2001.

Simmons, Marc, *Massacre on the Lordsburg Road*, College Station: Texas A&M University Press, 1997.

Sladen, Joseph Alton, and Sweeney, Edwin R., *Making Peace with Cochise*, Norman: University of Oklahoma Press, 1997.

Sweeney, Edwin R., *Mangas Coloradas*, Norman: University of Oklahoma Press, 1998.

Sweeney, Edwin R., *Cochise*, Norman: University of Oklahoma Press, 1991.

Thrapp, Dan L., *The Conquest of Apacheria*, Norman: University of Oklahoma Press, 1967.

Thrapp, Dan L., *Victorio and the Mimbres Apaches*, Norman: University of Oklahoma Press, 1974.

Thrapp, Dan L., *Al Sieber, Chief of Scouts*, Norman: University of Oklahoma Press, 1964.

Weber, David J., *The Taos Trappers*, Norman: University of Oklahoma Press, 1968.

ABOUT THE AUTHOR

Steve Price has been a full-time writer and photographer for more than five decades, specializing in outdoor recreation, travel, American history, and nature photography. He has written more than 3,500 magazine articles for dozens of publications, several video scripts, and seventeen books on subjects ranging from freshwater fishing to African wildlife to Spanish mustangs. His photography has won national and international awards and been used by the National Geographic Society, the Ford Motor Company, the Rocky Mountain Elk Foundation, and many others. He has traveled widely throughout the world, and currently serves as a contributing editor for *Field & Stream* and as a columnist for the Yamaha Marine Group. In 2010 he was inducted into the Bass Fishing Hall of Fame, and in 2017 into the Legends of the Outdoors Hall of Fame. He recently relocated from his home in New Mexico, where he worked with the Apaches, to Mena, Arkansas.

Index